To:

_____

From:

_____

Date:

_____

My
Pocket
Prayer Partner
for Moms

HOWARD BOOKS
A DIVISION OF SIMON & SCHUSTER
New York   London   Toronto   Sydney

Our purpose at Howard Books is to:
- Increase faith in the hearts of growing Christians
- Inspire holiness in the lives of believers
- Instill hope in the hearts of struggling people everywhere
  Because He's coming again!

Published by Howard Books, a division of Simon & Schuster, Inc.
1230 Avenue of the Americas, New York, NY 10020
www.howardpublishing.com

My Pocket Prayer Partner for Moms © 2007 by Dave Bordon and Associates, LLC

Library of Congress Cataloging-in-Publication Data

My pocket prayer partner for moms / [edited by Chrys Howard].
    p. cm.
1. Mothers—Prayers and devotions. I. Howard, Chrys, 1953-
BV4847.M9 2007
242'.6431—dc22

2007014983

ISBN-13: 978- 1-4165-4216-2
ISBN-10:   1-4165-4216-7
10 9 8 7 6 5 4 3 2 1

ISBN-13: 978- 1-58229-691-3 (gift edition)
ISBN-10:   1-58229-691-X (gift edition)
10 9 8 7 6 5 4 3 2 1

HOWARD and colophon are registered trademarks of Simon & Schuster, Inc.

Manufactured in China

For information regarding special discounts for bulk purchases, please contact:
Simon & Schuster Special Sales at 1-800-456-6798 or business@simonandschuster.com.

Project developed by Bordon Books, Tulsa, Oklahoma
Project writing and compilation by Christy Phillippe, Betsy Williams, Rayné Bordon, and Shawna McMurry in association with Bordon Books
Edited by Chrys Howard
Cover design by Bordon Books
Permissions acknowledgments are on pages 216–217.

Contents

A prayer concerning . . .

Introduction

Life for moms in today's culture is stressful to say the least. Juggling kids and schedules amid an already busy life that includes a job and housework leaves most with very little energy or enthusiasm.

If the above description sounds like your lifestyle, then *My Pocket Prayer Partner for Moms* is just for you. It was designed to be a helpful resource in your daily walk with the Lord. With fifty topics ranging from discovering peace, receiving God's guidance, and tackling conflict in the home to God's healing of your child—you will find answers for your specific everyday needs. It is full of heartfelt prayers to help you connect to God and talk to Him about your life. Each topic covered will also include a short reflection and on-target promises from God's Word, as well as journaling space for you to record your thoughts or God's answers to your prayers. In the back of the book there is a daily Bible reading guide to help you incorporate God's Word into your daily routine.

As you take the time to enter God's presence, you will be inspired and challenged to see your situation from God's perspective and turn it over to Him. So whatever your need may be, pour your heart out to the One who loves you most. He is waiting!

Tips for Having a Great Quiet Time

You may feel that the last thing you need is another commitment, but spending time with God is worth the effort. He desires to guide you, He wants to comfort you in the hard times, and He wants to be your friend. But He can do that only if you spend time with Him. The Bible says, "Draw near to God and He will draw near to you" (James 4:8 NKJV). Why not decide today that you will make Him a priority?

Here are some helpful tips:

- Give God your undivided attention. Find a quiet place where you and God can meet.

- Schedule a specific time. You are more likely to follow through.

- Read some verses from the Bible. Choose an easy-to-read translation. (You may want to use the Bible reading plan on pages 204–215.) As you start to read the Bible, ask the Holy Spirit to speak to your heart. As He impresses your heart and mind with His Word, why not pray those scriptures back to God? You may want to personalize those verses or paraphrase them in your own words. Praying God's Word back to Him is just one way that you can communicate with God.

- As you pray, also ask God for what you need. Keep a journal and record all the answers to your prayers. This will encourage you when you are down.

- The book of Psalms instructs us to sing to the Lord. Get a praise CD and sing along with it to your Heavenly Father.

- Talk to Him as you would a friend, from your heart. Then listen to see what He is saying to you. Remember, it is a relationship—it's not just you asking for stuff.

- If this is new to you, start out small, perhaps fifteen minutes. When you form the habit, you'll want to increase the time. As you get to know God even better, spending time with Him will go from discipline to desire to delight.

This book you hold in your hands is full of on-target promises from God's Word, heartfelt prayers on real-life topics, journaling prompts, and encouraging meditations that you can use as a helpful resource in your quiet time with God.

Anger

Dear God,

I am so angry that I'm about to explode! But that would only make the situation worse. I know how destructive anger is, and I don't want to say or do anything that I will later regret or that would displease You.

On the other hand, suppressing these powerful emotions would be harmful to me mentally and physically, and that would not please You either. Father, give me wisdom on how to deal with this situation in a healthy, godly manner that will honor You and set a good example for my children.

In Jesus' name,
Amen.

When you are angry, do not sin. And do not go on being angry all day. Do not give the devil a way to defeat you.

EPHESIANS 4:26–27 ICB

Human anger does not achieve God's righteous purpose.

JAMES 1:20 GNT

He who is slow to anger is better than the mighty,
And he who rules his spirit than he who takes a city.

PROVERBS 16:32 NKJV

Hot tempers start fights;
a calm, cool spirit keeps the peace.

PROVERBS 15:18 MSG

A fool gives full vent to anger,
but the wise quietly holds it back.

PROVERBS 29:11 NRSV

Don't ever forget that it is best to listen much, speak little, and not become angry.

JAMES 1:19 TLB

When angry, count ten before you speak;
if very angry, an hundred.

THOMAS JEFFERSON

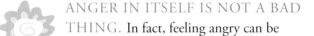 ANGER IN ITSELF IS NOT A BAD THING. In fact, feeling angry can be healthy. It can alert you that a boundary has been violated and lets you know that a situation needs to be dealt with.

As a parent, you will have plenty of opportunities to get peeved at your children. And that's okay. But it's not okay to take that anger out on them. That is when anger turns to sin.

The next time you feel that emotion bubbling up within you, try this. First, count to ten or whatever you need to do to get a grip on yourself. Leave the room if you have to. Next, when you are reasonably calm, pray and ask the Lord how to handle the situation. Since God has an abundance of wisdom and deals with unruly children as a way of life, He certainly can help. Let God speak His peace into your own heart before you confront your children. Finally, talk to them. In a calm manner, tell them you feel anger toward them and tell them why. Then tell them what you expect from them and end on a positive note such as a prayer or a hug.

This may sound simplistic, but God's Word always works. He says when there is a conflict between you and another person, you should go to them and resolve it. When you do this, you are teaching your children by example how to deal with anger in their own lives. Will you give it a try?

Is there something between you and one of your children right now that needs to be dealt with? How will you resolve it?

_____

_____

_____

_____

_____

_____

_____

_____

_____

_____

_____

_____

_____

_____

_____

_____

Anxiety

Heavenly Father,

Anxiety is weighing heavily on me, and my insides are tied up in knots. Even my children sense something is wrong.

I know I shouldn't worry, because You stand ready to take my burdens. And You can do something about them! So right now, I choose to cast my cares on You, and I ask You to help me not to take them back. I receive Your peace to replace anxiety and focus my thoughts on You and Your promises. Thank You for taking care of this situation for me. You are faithful.

In Jesus' name,
Amen.

May God bless you richly and grant you increasing
freedom from all anxiety and fear.

1 Peter 1:2 tlb

I am filled with trouble and anxiety,
but your commandments bring me joy.

Psalm 119:143 gnt

Anxiety in a man's heart weighs it down,
But a good word makes it glad.

Proverbs 12:25 nasb

When anxiety was great within me,
your consolation brought joy to my soul.

Psalm 94:19 niv

Do not be anxious about anything,
but in everything, by prayer and petition,
with thanksgiving, present your requests to God. And the
peace of God, which transcends all understanding, will
guard your hearts and your minds in Christ Jesus.

Philippians 4:6–7 niv

*Anxiety is the rust of life, destroying its brightness and weaken-
ing its power. A childlike and abiding trust in Providence is its
best preventive and remedy.*

Tryon Edwards

AS A MOM, YOU'RE EXPECTED TO HAVE EVERYTHING TOGETHER— to be the one in charge. Yet when you're facing difficult situations in your own life, being in charge is the last thing you feel like doing. You'd much rather be taken care of than be the caretaker. You don't want to take your frustrations out on your children or transfer your anxiety to them, yet it's difficult to go about the day pretending that nothing is wrong. So how do you handle these trying times?

First Peter 5:7 NIV gives this advice: "Cast all your anxiety on [the Lord] because he cares for you." No matter how harried life may seem at the time, don't neglect your prayer time with God. Take a few moments of alone time with Him, pouring out your heart to Him. Allow Him to comfort you and sooth your hurting heart. Not only will you feel better and have the strength needed to go about the day, but your children will feel the effects of your prayer time as well.

If your children can still detect your anxiety, be honest with them. They may not need to know all the details, but share with them what you can. Let them know that they are not to blame for your worry and allow them to be a comfort to you. If you can, use this time as an opportunity to share God's promises with your children.

Read Psalm 55:22 NIV together: "Cast your cares on the LORD and he will sustain you; he will never let the righteous fall."

List some cares in your life that you need to surrender to God.

_____

_____

_____

_____

_____

_____

_____

_____

_____

_____

_____

_____

_____

_____

_____

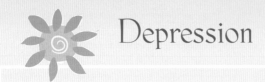

Depression

Father,

I'm more than just blue—I'm suffering from a full-blown case of depression, and I can't seem to shake it. Everything looks gray, and I feel numb inside. Will I ever be joyful again?

Hold me in Your arms, Father, and comfort me. Reassure me of Your love and concern. I give You the seemingly hopeless situations and ask You to work Your miracles. How wonderful it is to know that I am not alone. You are always with me—never judging, but always full of hope and encouragement. I put my trust in You.

In Jesus' name,
Amen.

I am standing here depressed and gloomy, but I will
meditate upon your kindness to this lovely land. . . .
O my soul, don't be discouraged. Don't be upset.
Expect God to act! For I know that I shall again have
plenty of reason to praise him for all that he will do.
He is my help! He is my God!

PSALM 42:6, 11 TLB

He will not break the bruised reed, nor quench the dimly
burning flame. He will encourage the fainthearted, those
tempted to despair.

ISAIAH 42:3 TLB

"The eternal God is your refuge,
and underneath are the everlasting arms."

DEUTERONOMY 33:27 NIV

"I called to the LORD in my distress,
and he answered me.
From the depths of my [watery] grave I cried for help,
and you heard my cry."

JONAH 2:2 GWT

*Jesus understands like no one else. He will lead you through
the darkness and into the light.*

JOSEPH GRIMALDI IS REMEM-
BERED AS ONE OF HISTORY'S
GREATEST CLOWNS. He was exclusively
a theatrical clown, and he is considered the "Father of
Modern Clowning" because he is the entertainer who el-
evated the white-faced clown to a starring role. He played
for the King of England, among others, and he seemed to
make the whole world laugh.

So great was Joseph Grimaldi's reputation that a doctor
once gave a patient who was suffering from depression this
simple prescription: "You must go to the music hall and
see Grimaldi."

The patient bowed and said, "I'm sorry, doctor, but
with me that will not work. You see, I am Grimaldi."

Depression is a common problem for most people—
even moms! Life can seem to be filled with problems that
can become overwhelming at times. But God's Word has
the answer for depression: "The joy of the LORD is your
strength" (Nehemiah 8:10 NIV). The joy of the Lord is
not a temporary amusement, such as the performance of
a white-faced clown, but it is a lasting, abiding sense that
everything will be okay, because God is still in charge.

Whatever problems are weighing you down, whatever
feelings of hopelessness or helplessness you may be experiencing, you can still begin to experience the joy of the

Lord. Tell God how you are feeling, and ask Him to bring
His peace and comfort back into your life. In response,
He will bless you—and your children—with His presence,
which is filled with joy: "You will show me the path of life;
in Your presence is fullness of joy; at Your right hand are
pleasures forevermore" (Psalm 16:11 NKJV).

How can you experience more of God's joy?

# Disappointment

Father in Heaven,

I can't believe this has happened. I had such high hopes, and now they have been dashed. How did this happen? What now?

You are the God of hope, so I set my gaze on You. Replace my disappointment with Your comfort, and use this situation to give me fresh insight and to help me grow. Show me where my expectations were unrealistic or where my hope became misplaced.

I have been let down, but this isn't the end. Lead me out of disappointment and help me get back on track.

In Jesus' name,
Amen.

Unrelenting disappointment leaves you heartsick,
but a sudden good break can turn life around.

PROVERBS 13:12 MSG

The LORD looks after those who fear him,
those who put their hope in his love.

PSALM 33:18 NCV

Trust in Him at all times, you people;
Pour out your heart before Him;
God is a refuge for us.

PSALM 62:8 NKJV

Blessed be the God and Father of our Lord Jesus Christ,
the Father of mercies and the God of all consolation.

2 CORINTHIANS 1:3 NRSV

God our Father loves us.
He is kind and has given us eternal comfort and
a wonderful hope. We pray that our Lord Jesus Christ and
God our Father will encourage you and help you.

2 THESSALONIANS 2:16–17 CEV

*Never forget: God is a God of miracles. He can turn even the
biggest disappointments into something beautiful.*

A YOUNG MAN ONCE CALLED UP HIS GIRLFRIEND TO INVITE HER ON AN IMPORTANT DATE. Something very special was about to happen, he assured her. She dressed carefully to look her best and waited nervously for the time of their date to arrive. The young man picked her up that evening in his antique jalopy, and as they drove along, he was quiet, obviously deep in thought.

Finally, the silence was broken—the young man enthusiastically told his girlfriend that the big event was near. Anticipating a marriage proposal, she could scarcely contain her excitement.

At last, he declared: "The great moment has arrived!" He watched, overjoyed, as the car's odometer slowly passed the 100,000-mile mark. Almost delirious with excitement, he exclaimed: "Look! Everything is back to zero!"

The girl grimaced. "Back to zero is right," she said.

Life can be disappointing at times—especially when we place our hope, trust, and expectations in other people, including our spouses or children. As a mom, it is difficult not to have high hopes for your kids, but sometimes disappointment is the result. At such times, it's easy to feel discouraged, even as if you are "back to zero." But those are the times to remember that God has a plan for your children and your family—and He is still in charge! He can even work something out for good that doesn't seem good at the time. Disappointments may come, but there is One whose promises hold true—both for you and for your kids—and He will never let you down.

What unrealistic expectations may you have set for your children?

_____

_____

_____

_____

_____

_____

_____

_____

_____

_____

_____

_____

_____

Fear

Heavenly Father,

This world can be such a scary place. I'm not as concerned about myself as I am my children—there is only so much I can do to protect them.

Thankfully, I can count on You to do what I cannot do. I ask You to cover us with Your presence and assign angels to protect and deliver us. Teach us to recognize Your voice so that when danger is near, we hear You telling us where to go and what to do. You are our refuge, our place of safety and protection.

In Jesus' name,

Amen.

"The Lord himself will go before you.
He will be with you. He will not leave you or forget you.
Don't be afraid. Don't worry."

Deuteronomy 31:8 icb

"I am the Lord, your God,
who takes hold of your right hand
and says to you, Do not fear;
I will help you."

Isaiah 41:13 niv

Say to those who are of a fearful heart,
"Be strong, do not fear!
Here is your God. . . .
He will come and save you."

Isaiah 35:4 nrsv

Fear not [there is nothing to fear], for I am with you; do
not look around you in terror and be dismayed, for I am
your God. I will strengthen and harden you to difficulties,
yes, I will help you; yes, I will hold you up.

Isaiah 41:10 amp

*Even when we are not aware of it,
the Father is watching over and protecting us.*

THE EARLY AMERICAN INDIANS HAD A UNIQUE PRACTICE OF TRAINING YOUNG BRAVES. On the night of a boy's thirteenth birthday, after learning hunting, scouting, and fishing skills, he was put to one final test. He was placed in a dense forest to spend the entire night alone.

Until then, he had never been away from the security of the family and tribe. But on this night, he was blindfolded and taken several miles away. When he took off the blindfold, he was in the middle of thick woods, and he was terrified. Every time a twig snapped, he visualized a wild animal ready to pounce. After what seemed like an eternity, dawn broke, and the first rays of sunlight entered the interior of the forest. Looking around, the boy saw flowers, trees, and the outline of a path. Then, to his utter astonishment, he beheld the figure of a man standing just a few feet away, armed with bow and arrow. It was his father. He had been there all night long.

What fear are you facing today? Perhaps it involves the health of one of your children or family members. It might concern a lack of finances or a conflict in the family. Whatever it is, you should know that you are not alone. Your Heavenly Father stands ready to protect and comfort you. And unlike the American Indian father, He is not standing in the bushes, waiting for the daybreak to reveal Himself. Rather, He is right by your side, defending you from whatever might come your way.

What is your greatest fear? How can you turn it over to God?

_____

_____

_____

_____

_____

_____

_____

_____

_____

_____

_____

_____

_____

_____

_____

Grief

Dear Lord,

My heart is agonizing over this loss. In fact, grief has so consumed me that I wonder if I will ever experience joy and laughter again. Everything in me wants to run from this pain, to do something—anything—so that I won't feel it anymore, but I know that lasting comfort can be found only in You. Anything else will provide only temporary relief and prolong the healing process.

I run to You, Father. Hold me in Your loving, compassionate, healing embrace. Guide my journey to restoration that I may smile again.

In Jesus' name,
Amen.

[Jesus said,] "I tell you the truth, you will weep and mourn.
. . . You will grieve, but your grief will turn to joy."

John 16:20 niv

You changed my sorrow into dancing.
You took away my clothes of sadness,
and clothed me in happiness.

Psalm 30:11 ncv

Blessed are they that mourn: for they shall be comforted.

Matthew 5:4 kjv

The ransomed of the Lord shall return,
and come to Zion with singing;
everlasting joy shall be upon their heads;
they shall obtain joy and gladness,
and sorrow and sighing shall flee away.

Isaiah 35:10 nrsv

The Lord is near to the brokenhearted,
and saves the crushed in spirit.

Psalm 34:18 nrsv

*What greater comfort can there be than that provided by the
Comforter, the Holy Spirit of God?*

DR. R. A. TORREY, DEAN OF THE BIBLE INSTITUTE OF LOS ANGE-LES, lost his twelve-year-old daughter in an accident. The funeral was on a rainy day. It was dark and dismal as they stood there beside that hole in the ground, surrounded by loved ones. Mrs. Torrey said to her husband, "I'm so glad Elizabeth is not in that box." Their grief went home with them that night as they tried to sleep.

Dr. Torrey got up in the morning and went for a walk. A wave of grief broke over him anew, the loneliness of his daughter's absence, the terrible feeling of knowing they would never hear her laughter again, never see her face, never witness her growth. He couldn't take it. And so he leaned against the streetlight, looked up, and began to pray. This is what he experienced: "Just then the fountain, the Holy Spirit, whom I had in my heart, broke forth with such power as I think I had never experienced before. And it was the most joyful moment I had ever known in my life! It is an unspeakably glorious thing to have within you a fountain ever springing up, springing up, springing up, ever springing up 365 days in every year, springing up under all circumstances."

No matter what has caused your grief, the comfort of the Holy Spirit can be yours. Jesus "has borne our griefs and carried our sorrows" (Isaiah 53:4 NKJV), and God himself will comfort us when we need it: "God and Father of our Lord Jesus Christ . . . is the source of every mercy and the God who comforts us. He comforts us in all our troubles" (2 Corinthians 1:3–4 NLT [96]). Run into the arms of your Heavenly Father and feel His comfort today.

How can Jesus help you bear your sorrows?

_____

_____

_____

_____

_____

_____

_____

_____

_____

_____

_____

_____

_____

_____

_____

Loneliness

Father,

I feel so alone right now—even when I am around other people. What I am needing is a heart-to-heart connection with another person, not just another warm body in the room.

Thankfully I am never really alone, for You are always with me. You are the friend who sticks closer than a brother. As I draw near to You, hold me close to Your heart. Comfort my soul and fill up this aching loneliness.

I do need human companionship as well, so lead me to people with whom I can enjoy fellowship and laughter.

In Jesus' name,
Amen.

My eyes are always looking to the Lord for help. . . .
Turn to me and be kind to me.
I am lonely and hurting.

Psalm 25:15–16 icb

Two are better than one,
because they have a good return for their work:
If one falls down,
his friend can help him up.
But pity the man who falls
and has no one to help him up!

Ecclesiastes 4:9–10 niv

You listened and pulled me
from a lonely pit
full of mud and mire.
You . . . gave me a new song.

Psalm 40:1–3 cev

You should not stay away from the church meetings,
as some are doing, but you should meet together
and encourage each other.

Hebrews 10:25 ncv

Loneliness is the first thing that God's eye nam'd not good.

John Milton

ACCORDING TO A RECENT STUDY conducted by doctors in Sweden, lonely people seem more likely to die of heart disease than do the socially active. The study allowed for medical and lifestyle risk factors—age, smoking, physical inactivity, and signs of heart disease—and found that the subjects with fewer social contacts had a 40 percent greater risk of dying from cardiovascular disease than the rest did.

"Loneliness," a similar study reported, "can speed your demise no matter how conscientiously you care for your body." One study of elderly heart attack patients found that those with two or more close associates enjoyed twice the one-year survival rate of those who were completely alone. "We go through life surrounded by protective convoys of others," says Robert Kahn, a University of Michigan psychologist who has studied the health effects of companionship. "People who manage to maintain a network of social support do best."

As a mom, even though you may be surrounded by your children all day long, it is still easy to become lonely and feel cut off from the outside world. God created you for social contact, however, and He knows when you need some time alone with your husband or a special night out with your friends.

Ask the Lord to help you maintain solid relationships

even in the midst of a hectic and busy lifestyle. And during those times when others can't be there for you, He will. F. B. Meyer once said, "Loneliness is an opportunity for Jesus to make Himself known." Invite Him to share the ups and downs of your daily life with you, and you will never be alone.

What do you do when you feel lonely?

_____

_____

_____

_____

_____

_____

_____

_____

_____

_____

_____

_____

_____

Rejection

Father,

Nothing hurts quite like the sting of rejection, and I've been stung. It makes me feel defective . . . unlovable . . . less than adequate.

I'm so thankful that You will never reject me. You love me just the way I am—warts and all. There's such comfort in that. Plus, You know what it feels like to be rejected, so I know You understand.

Wrap me in Your arms, Lord, and heal this wound. Help me to respond to rejection the way that You do, and help me see myself through Your eyes.

In Jesus' name,
Amen.

[Jesus said,] "Those the Father has given me will come to me, and I will never reject them."

JOHN 6:37 NLT (96)

Do not reject me or forsake me,
O God my Savior.
Though my father and mother forsake me,
the LORD will receive me.

PSALM 27:9–10 NIV

[Jesus said,] "He who listens to you listens to me;
he who rejects you rejects me; but he who rejects me
rejects him who sent me."

LUKE 10:16 NIV

The LORD will not reject his people;
he will never forsake his inheritance.

PSALM 94:14 NIV

For the sake of his great name the LORD will not reject
his people, because the LORD was pleased
to make you his own.

1 SAMUEL 12:22 NIV

Your Heavenly Father will never, ever reject you.
He accepts you just the way you are . . . period.

EVERYONE KNOWS WHAT IT FEELS LIKE to be criticized and rejected, often by the very people in our lives we love the most. At some point in our lives, we all have been ignored, overlooked, or rejected by parents and friends—even our children.

However, although other people may reject us, God never will. The acceptance of God is not based on who we are or what we can do—it is instead based entirely on His kindness and mercy: "When the kindness of God our Savior and His love for mankind appeared, He saved us, not on the basis of deeds which we have done in righteousness, but according to His mercy" (Titus 3:4–5 NASB).

It's easy to get defensive or angry when it seems that other people are turning their backs on us. Our human nature wants others to love us and to respect us. Sadly, this does not always happen. But the good news is that we have a Heavenly Father who accepts us and who teaches us to accept others in return.

Rather than rejecting you, Jesus accepts you—just as you are! God doesn't view us from a "human" perspective—He views us instead through the shed blood of His Son, Jesus, and He asks that we forgive those who reject us, just as He has forgiven us.

If you are feeling left out or left behind, remember that Jesus knows how you feel—and He cares. Jesus was "despised and rejected by men," as well (see Isaiah 53:3 NIV), and He longs to put His arms of comfort and acceptance around you today.

Have you felt rejected lately? Ask the Lord to remind you of a few things He has done for you that prove His love.

Stress

Heavenly Father,

The stress is off the charts—I'm about to pull my hair out! To make matters worse, the children sense my stress and then act out. There never seems to be enough time or energy to get everything done. Can we please get off this merry-go-round?

Forgive me, Father, for falling into panic mode. It's totally unproductive and makes life unpleasant for everyone. Right now, I give You my entire load. Refresh me as I bask in Your presence. Be my administrator and help me to prioritize. Lead me in the path of peace.

In the name of Your Son, the Prince of Peace,

Amen.

[Jesus said,] "Are you tired? Worn out? . . . Get away with me and you'll recover your life. I'll show you how to take a real rest. Walk with me and work with me—watch how I do it. Learn the unforced rhythms of grace. I won't lay anything heavy or ill-fitting on you. Keep company with me and you'll learn to live freely and lightly."

MATTHEW 11:28–30 MSG

"Times of refreshing . . . come from the presence of the Lord."

ACTS 3:20 NRSV

[The Lord says,] "I will refresh the weary and satisfy the faint."

JEREMIAH 31:25 NIV

"I, your GOD, have a firm grip on you and I'm not letting go. I'm telling you, 'Don't panic. I'm right here to help you.'"

ISAIAH 41:13 MSG

Don't fret or worry. . . . Let petitions and praises shape your worries into prayers, letting God know your concerns.

PHILIPPIANS 4:6 MSG

Need a tranquilizer? Try the green pastures and still waters of the Good Shepherd.

THE STRESS DIET

Breakfast: ½ grapefruit; 1 piece whole-wheat toast; 8 oz. skim milk

Lunch: 4 oz. lean broiled chicken breast; 1 cup steamed zucchini; 1 Oreo cookie; herbal tea

Mid-afternoon snack: Rest of the package of Oreo cookies; 1 qt. rocky road ice cream; 1 jar hot fudge

Dinner: 2 loaves garlic bread; large mushroom and pepperoni pizza; large pitcher root beer; 3 Milky Ways; entire frozen cheesecake, eaten directly from the freezer

As a mom, you have probably had days like this, in which the stresses begin to pile up and by the end of the day you are frazzled and exhausted—and ready for cheesecake!

But God has a better way to deal with stress, and that is to take all your cares and worries to Him and receive His rest and peace in return. The Bible says, "[Cast] all your care upon Him, for He cares for you" (1 Peter 5:7 NKJV).

Jesus instructs us in Matthew 11:29–30 NLT, "Take my yoke upon you. Let me teach you, because I am humble and gentle at heart, and you will find rest for your souls. For my yoke is easy to bear, and the burden I give you is light."

No matter what you are dealing with today, you can

go to Jesus and give Him all the stresses and burdens you are carrying. Let Him take them from you. After all, His shoulders are bigger than yours. Instead, take a deep breath and relax, knowing that He is in charge and has your best interests at heart, and He will work everything out in His timing and plan.

What is your greatest source of stress? How can it be relieved?

Temptation

Heavenly Father,

I need You in a big way. This temptation that is being leveled against me is strong, and I am afraid I might give in.

I run to You, Father, because You are my refuge, my very present help in trouble. As I draw near to You, fill me with Your grace and strength to stand against this trick of the enemy. Deliver me from evil and lead me to the place of safety and triumph. Help me to be a good example to my children as through Christ You enable me to overcome.

In the name of Jesus,
Amen.

Let no one say when he is tempted, "I am being tempted by God"; for God cannot be tempted by evil, and He Himself does not tempt anyone. But each one is tempted when he is carried away and enticed by his own lust.

JAMES 1:13–14 NASB

We are not ignorant about Satan's scheming.

2 CORINTHIANS 2:11 GWT

Give yourselves completely to God. Stand against the devil, and the devil will run from you.

JAMES 4:7 NCV

The temptations in your life are no different from what others experience. And God is faithful. He will not allow the temptation to be more than you can stand. When you are tempted, he will show you a way out so that you can endure.

1 CORINTHIANS 10:13 NLT

Because Jesus experienced temptation when he suffered, he is able to help others when they are tempted.

HEBREWS 2:18 GWT

Temptations are cleverly disguised substitutes for the only true source of satisfaction—God himself.

"WHAT ARE YOU DOING, SON?" THE SHOPKEEPER ASKED A LITTLE BOY whose eyes were on a large basket of apples outside the storefront. "Are you trying to steal one of those apples?"

"No sir," replied the boy. "I'm trying not to."

Temptation can come in many forms. A magazine once asked its readers to rank the areas of greatest spiritual challenge to them. The results came back in this order: (1) materialism, (2) pride, (3) self-centeredness, (4) laziness, (5) (tie between) anger/bitterness and sexual lust, (6) envy, (7) gluttony, and (8) lying. Respondents also noted that temptations were more potent when they neglected their time with God and when they were physically tired. On the other hand, successful resistance was accomplished by prayer, avoiding compromising situations, Bible study, and being accountable to someone else.

Even though you are trying to set a good example for your children, you may still struggle with temptation. But you have a greater chance of winning over temptation when you follow the proven steps: Stay close to God through prayer and Bible study; stay away from whatever is tempting you; and find an accountability partner. When you do all the things that you can do to avoid temptation and keep from sin, God will honor your willingness to obey Him and give you the strength you need to stand strong.

You may have temptations—but they don't have to have you! Temptations will surely come, but they can be an opportunity for you to rely on God's strength to deliver you.

What is your area of greatest temptation?

_____

_____

_____

_____

_____

_____

_____

_____

_____

_____

_____

_____

_____

_____

Contentment

Father in Heaven,

Teaching my children to be content is challenging. It's hard enough for me to be satisfied when "keeping up with the Joneses" has practically become a national pastime and advertising bombards us continually.

Forgive us for the times we have been discontent. You have been so good to us, and I thank You for every blessing we enjoy. Help me to instill this same thankfulness in my children. I want eternal, spiritual values to be the top priorities in our home—You first, people next, and "things" last—for godliness with contentment is great gain.

In Jesus' name,
Amen.

[Jesus] told the people, "Be careful to guard yourselves from every kind of greed. Life is not about having a lot of material possessions."

Luke 12:15 gwt

There is great gain in godliness
combined with contentment.

1 Timothy 6:6 nrsv

I say it is better to be content
with what little you have.
Otherwise, you will always be struggling for more,
and that is like chasing the wind.

Ecclesiastes 4:6 ncv

Because your love is better than life,
I will praise you. . . .
I will be content as if I had eaten the best foods.

Psalm 63:3,5 ncv

Keep your lives free from the love of money
and be content with what you have.

Hebrews 13:5 niv

Contentment is a pearl of great price, and whoever procures it at the expense of ten thousand desires makes a wise and a happy purchase.

John Balguy

THE WORD CONTENTMENT
DOESN'T GET MUCH USE TODAY!
We feel we need everything—more and
bigger and better. We are bombarded daily with TV ads
that say we must have things in order to be fulfilled.
And we want the intangibles, too—power, fame, and
success. We want it all! And then we'll be happy.

This message is being relayed to our children loud and
clear. As a parent, it is up to us to counteract this worldly
message with truth. God says that we brought nothing
into the world and we cannot take anything out of it either
(1 Timothy 6:7). Therefore, we should be content if we
have food and clothing. This really gets to the heart of this
issue. Our life doesn't consist of things. Besides, this earth
is not our real home anyway, if we are Christians. We are
to lay up treasures in Heaven, not on earth.

Certainly, it's hard for children to comprehend this
"heavenly" message while living in a prosperous nation
surrounded by friends who get all the latest gizmos
and gadgets. But that's where you come in. Your attitude toward material things will rub off on them. Do
they see you striving and working longer hours just to
have more? Or do they see you being less interested in
"things" and more interested in what's really important—God and friends and family?

One of the best remedies for discontentment is gratitude—being thankful for the things you do have instead of focusing on what you don't have. Teach your children an attitude of gratitude. As they see you expressing thanks for even the little things, they too will become grateful.

Have your kids write down ten things they're thankful for. You make a list, too, and then read them aloud to each other.

Endurance

Heavenly Father,

Some days it seems that all I do is run, run, run—doing things for my children and taking care of my other responsibilities. At times I wonder how much longer I can keep up this pace. My endurance level is running low.

Have I taken on too much? If so, show me what activities I need to curtail. Teach me to follow Your lead and commit only to what You desire me to do. Even then, I need Your grace, power, and strength to endure to the end. Help me to do it with joy.

In Jesus' name,
Amen.

His glorious power will make you patient and strong
enough to endure anything, and you will be truly happy.

COLOSSIANS 1:11 CEV

Those who trust in the LORD are like Mount Zion,
which cannot be shaken but endures forever.

PSALM 125:1 NIV

You need endurance so that after you have done what God
wants you to do, you can receive what he has promised.

HEBREWS 10:36 GWT

He gives power to the faint,
and strengthens the powerless.
Even youths will faint and be weary,
and the young will fall exhausted;
but those who wait for the LORD shall renew their strength,
they shall mount up with wings like eagles,
they shall run and not be weary,
they shall walk and not faint.

ISAIAH 40:29–31 NRSV

*God never commissioned us to run the rat race. The race that
God assigns comes with the power to endure.*

❋

DOES YOUR LIFE EVER FEEL LIKE A MARATHON, racing from one commitment to another? Between meetings, school events, practices, games, recitals, and the many other activities moms are expected to participate in, there's little time for personal reflection. When your life is feeling a little overwhelming, try the following steps:

1. Stop. Psalm 46:10 nkjv exhorts us to simply "Be still, and know that I am God." Acknowledging that God is in control—not us—can bring great relief and liberty to our lives.

2. Refocus. Philippians 3:13–14 niv outlines a great plan for running life's race: "Forgetting what is behind and straining toward what is ahead, I press on toward the goal to win the prize for which God has called me heavenward." Are all of your activities in line with your goals? If not, maybe it's time to make some changes. Perhaps you make a point to attend all of your children's ball games to foster confidence in them, but you participate in PTA to gain the approval of your peers. By measuring each of your activities according to your goals, you'll find out what's most important to you, and you will be able to give those activities the attention they deserve.

3. Run. Hebrews 12:1 niv says: "Let us run with

perseverance the race marked out for us." Once you have a clear vision of why you participate in your daily activities, it will be much easier to do them with all your heart, to press through your tiredness, and to enjoy your life.

List your daily activities and the goals they fulfill. If there are any that don't line up with your goals, consider eliminating them from your schedule.

_____

_____

_____

_____

_____

_____

_____

_____

_____

_____

_____

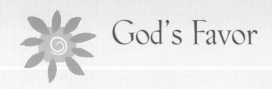

God's Favor

Heavenly Father,

What a blessing it is to have Your favor! I realize it is because Jesus bore the penalty for my sin, and I do not take that for granted. In and of myself I am severely limited, but having Your favor supernaturally opens doors of opportunity and blessing to me. May it continue!

I pray that You will surround my children with favor as well—favor with their teachers, coaches, peers, and even their enemies. I will be quick to remind them that it is Your favor that crowns their lives with success.

In Your Son's name,
Amen.

The grace (blessing and favor) of the Lord Jesus Christ
(the Messiah) be with your spirit.

PHILEMON 1:25 AMP

The good obtain favor from the LORD.

PROVERBS 12:2 NRSV

The LORD God is a sun and shield;
the LORD bestows favor and honor;
no good thing does he withhold
from those whose walk is blameless.

PSALM 84:11 NIV

He prays to God and finds favor with him,
he sees God's face and shouts for joy;
he is restored by God to his righteous state.

JOB 33:26 NIV

[The Lord's] favor lasts a lifetime!

PSALM 30:5 NLT (96)

*God's favor opens doors that no man can shut and makes a
way where there seems to be no way.*

THE BIBLE SAYS GOD SURROUNDS HIS PEOPLE with favor as a shield (Psalm 5:12 NASB). What does a shield do? It protects and inspires confidence. God's favor can do the same, and He wants you to have it. When you ask for God's favor, your actions tell Him that you believe His intervention can make a difference, and it can.

Suppose you have an upcoming interview. Pray for favor with the person who will be interviewing you. If that job is the one for you, God can turn that person's heart toward you so that you are approved. It's not magic, but it is supernatural. It is God using His power to aid you along your journey.

But don't ever take it for granted. If God were to withdraw His favor from you, you would fail miserably. We must never think it is by our own wit or intellect or power that we achieve something. Even if we have wit and intellect, they, too, are gifts resulting from God's favor toward us. But as Christians, we should expect and look for God's favor.

In the Old Testament, Queen Esther prayed and fasted for favor with the king. If she showed up in his court without being summoned, she could be executed. But she needed to talk with him about the plot against the Jews, which called for their death. She knew that without God's favor, tragedy would result. She, therefore, sought favor, and favor she received. She not only received an audience with the king, but he also granted her request—the life of the Jews!

God hasn't changed—He will do the same for you. Why not ask for His favor today?

Do you or your children need God's favor today? Ask Him for it! When He answers the prayer, record the answer below.

_____

_____

_____

_____

_____

_____

_____

_____

_____

_____

Guidance

Father God,

I am not smart enough or wise enough to always know where to go, what to do, and when to do it; but You know all things, so I look to You for guidance. Thank You for sending the Holy Spirit to live inside me to help me. Teach me to recognize Your voice and to discern between it and my own thoughts. Guide me as I read the Bible, for Your words are alive. They are a lamp for my feet and a light for my path. Direct me to Your perfect will.

In Jesus' name,
Amen.

You light my lamp;
The LORD my God illumines my darkness.

PSALM 18:28 NASB

He leads the humble in justice,
And He teaches the humble His way.
All the paths of the LORD are lovingkindness and truth
to those who keep His covenant and His testimonies.

PSALM 25:9–10 NASB

He restores my soul;
He guides me in the paths of righteousness
For His name's sake.

PSALM 23:3 NASB

I will instruct you and teach you in the way
which you should go;
I will counsel you with My eye upon you.

PSALM 32: 8 NASB

The path of the righteous is like the light of dawn,
That shines brighter and brighter until the full day.

PROVERBS 4:18 NASB

*The Father is ever extending His hand to lead and guide us
into His best plans for our lives.*

ONE DAY WENDY DECIDED TO TAKE HER THREE CHILDREN to an ice-skating party in a nearby town. After several wrong turns and stops to ask directions, she finally pulled over to the side of the road and suggested that they all ask God to help them find the rink.

When Wendy and the kids finally arrived, they were nearly an hour late. The following week, however, as they all piled into the car to go skating again, her five-year-old son, Trenton, exclaimed: "Mom, let's pray now and save time!"

Sometimes it's hard to find our way through life. All of us face decisions that are often life-changing, but as parents, moms are responsible for more than just themselves. They are also responsible for the lives of their children—and so it's even more important to get God's perspective whenever an important choice presents itself.

Fortunately, God is always there to lead and guide us. The Bible says: "This great God is our God forever and ever. He will be our guide until we die" (Psalm 48:14 TLB). What an amazing promise! We have the assurance that God will show us the way to go—if we ask Him to.

The next time you are faced with a decision and need God's guidance, pray the prayer that King David prayed in the psalms: "Lord, lead me as you promised me you would. . . . Tell me clearly what to do, which way to turn" (Psalm 5:8 TLB). And then expect His answer to come!

In what areas do you need guidance from the Lord?

Healing

Dear Heavenly Father,

I come to You right now with a sick body that needs Your healing touch. You have revealed Yourself as my Great Physician and the Provider of everything I need.

Psalm 103 says that I should not forget Your many benefits, one of which is healing for my body. So, I am asking You to heal me now by Your almighty power. Please restore my strength so I can do the work You have called me to do and therefore glorify You. Thank You for hearing my prayer and making me whole.

In Jesus' name,
Amen.

[The Messiah] was wounded for our transgressions, he was bruised for our iniquities: the chastisement of our peace was upon him; and with his stripes we are healed.

Isaiah 53:5 kjv

"I am the Lord who heals you."

Exodus 15:26 nkjv

I will restore health unto thee, and I will heal thee of thy wounds, saith the Lord.

Jeremiah 30:17 kjv

[The Lord says,] Unto you that fear my name shall the Sun of righteousness arise with healing in his wings.

Malachi 4:2 kjv

Ye shall serve the Lord your God, and he shall bless thy bread, and thy water; and I will take sickness away from the midst of thee.

Exodus 23:25 kjv

Jesus is the same yesterday, today, and forever. He was and always will be the Great Physician.

JANET SNEEZED AND REACHED FOR THE TISSUE BOX on her desk.

Oh no, she murmured to herself. *I can't be coming down with a cold. I just can't be!* She had just been assigned a project that would require some overtime. And then there was Johnny, her son, whose Little League team was playing in a tournament. She couldn't miss that—he would be so disappointed.

As she continued sneezing, she silently prayed, "Lord, please touch me. I need Your healing." She then remembered the Bible story of a leper who went to Jesus. The leper bowed down in front of Jesus and said, "Lord, if You are willing, You can make me clean" (Matthew 8:2 NASB). He wasn't absolutely sure whether Jesus would want to heal him or not.

But Jesus gave him a clear answer. Jesus said, "I am willing; be cleansed" (v. 3). The Savior's words left no doubt that Jesus was indeed willing and wanted to heal him.

Do you ever doubt if God may want to do the same for you? The Bible says that Jesus is the same and that He never changes. Scriptures also say that God is not a respecter of persons, which means He plays no favorites. If He healed that man, He can also heal you.

Whether you have the flu or whether you have a more serious situation, God can help you. Since He goes to the trouble of keeping up with how many hairs you have on your head (Matthew 10:30), He surely cares when you are ill. Why not cry out to Him now. He is willing!

Write out a prayer to God asking Him for your healing. Then read it to Him. Thank Him for hearing your prayer and touching you.

Hope

Father in Heaven,

It seems I have come to a dead end, that hope is lost. Heaviness weighs on me, and a dark cloud has descended upon my mind. I cannot see the light at the end of the tunnel.

Thankfully, You are my light and my salvation. Open my eyes so that I can see what You see. You are the God of hope, and, with You, all things are possible. So I wait on You, Lord, to hear Your voice, to have my hope restored, to see Your goodness in the land of the living.

In the name of Your Son,
Amen.

May the God of hope fill you with all joy and peace in
believing, so that you will abound in hope
by the power of the Holy Spirit.

ROMANS 15:13 NASB

It is good both to hope and wait quietly for the
salvation of the Lord.

LAMENTATIONS 3:26 TLB

"The LORD is my portion," says my soul,
"Therefore I hope in Him!"
The LORD is good to those who wait for Him,
To the soul who seeks Him.

LAMENTATIONS 3:24–25 NKJV

No one whose hope is in you
will ever be put to shame.

PSALM 25:3 NIV

I will hope continually,
and will praise you yet more and more.
My mouth will tell of your righteous acts.

PSALM 71:14–15 NRSV

*Don't let the clouds of momentary setbacks cause you to
despair. The Son is ever shining. For the Christian, there are
always brighter days ahead.*

G. F. WATT HAS A FAMOUS PAINT-
ING TITLED *HOPE.* It pictures a poor
woman against the world. Her eyes are
bandaged so that she cannot see ahead. In her hands is
a harp, but all the strings are broken except one. Those
broken strings represent her shattered expectations, her
bitter disappointments. That one last unbroken string is
the string of hope. She strikes that string, and a glorious
melody floats out over the world; it fills her dark sky with
stars. The artist painted a great truth: Even when all else is
gone, you can still have hope.

Maybe you feel like that woman today. Maybe your
hopes and dreams are shattered and you think that nothing will ever be right again. God wants you to know that
there is always hope when you place your trust in Him.
He has great plans for you! "'I know the plans I have for
you,' declares the Lord, 'plans to prosper you and not to
harm you, plans to give you hope and a future'" (Jeremiah
29:11 NIV).

Someone once said, "Most of the important things in
the world have been accomplished by people who have
kept on trying when there seemed to be no hope at all."
If that's you—if you seem to have "no hope at all"—keep
on trying! Place your trust back where it belongs—in your
Heavenly Father—and know that He will work everything

out for your good (Romans 8:28). Hope is never lost when God is near.

How does your hope need to be renewed?

Joy

Heavenly Father,

Will You help me learn to be consistently joyful? Being up one day and down the next is not good for me, and it certainly doesn't make me fun to live with!

Since joy is a fruit of the Spirit, I know it is in me. Teach me how to walk in it moment by moment—to stay on top of my attitude so that I don't give in to negative thoughts and feelings. I want Your joy to be my strength so that I can truly be a light shining in this dark world.

In Jesus' name,
Amen.

Rejoice in the Lord always. Again I will say, rejoice!

PHILIPPIANS 4:4 NKJV

The ransomed of the LORD shall return,
And come to Zion with singing,
With everlasting joy on their heads.
They shall obtain joy and gladness;
Sorrow and sighing shall flee away.

ISAIAH 51:11 NKJV

You will go out with joy
and be led out in peace.
The mountains and hills will burst into song before you,
and all the trees in the fields will clap their hands.

ISAIAH 55:12 NCV

"The joy of the LORD is your strength."

NEHEMIAH 8:10 NASB

I will sing for joy about what your hands have done.

PSALM 92:4 NCV

Joy is to behold God in everything.

JULIAN OF NORWICH

JOY. THIS WORD IS OFTEN MIS-UNDERSTOOD. A lot of people think joy comes from having success or having everything you want. Of course that's not true because lots of people who have fame and fortune are not joyful.

Actually this word has less to do with outward circumstances and more to do with an attitude of the heart. The Bible talks about joy in connection with our relationship to God. We are to rejoice because we know Him, because He has saved us, because He will deliver us. And we can do this no matter what our outer circumstances are. The Apostle Paul was beaten and thrown into jail, yet did he sit in stocks crying? No. He sat in stocks rejoicing! (See Acts 16:25.) What did he have to rejoice about? He knew that there was another life after this one. He knew that one is only the rehearsal—the next life will last for eternity. He was living to please God, and even if he suffered as a result, it didn't matter. Why not? Because he would be rewarded in the next life. Also because he lived in the realization that his life belonged to God—his life had meaning.

In today's chaotic and unpredictable world, outward circumstances can never bring us joy. They're temporary. But in your heart, you can rejoice knowing that God loves you if you are His child. You can be happy that you will one day spend eternity with Him. And you will live in a place where there will be no more pain or sorrow or tears. Now, that's something to rejoice about!

Want to be joyful? Write down ten things for which you can be grateful and then fervently and lavishly thank God for each one. Joy will come.

Patience

Dear God,

Never have I needed patience like I have since becoming a mother. It is tested every day! I don't want to be sharp and impatient with my children because I know that harms their sensitive spirits.

The only way I can master patience is with Your assistance. Help me to find time to read Your Word and pray so that my spirit will be stronger than my emotions. Then, when opportunities arise to test me, help me to make that split-second decision to let Your patience rise up in me and win the battle.

In Jesus' name,
Amen.

We show that we are servants of God by
living a pure life, by our understanding,
by our patience, and by our kindness.

2 CORINTHIANS 6:6 ICB

Smart people are patient;
they will be honored if they ignore insults.

PROVERBS 19:11 NCV

Patient people have great understanding.

PROVERBS 14:29 NCV

Love is patient and kind.

1 CORINTHIANS 13:4 ICB

Always be humble and gentle.
Be patient and accept each other with love.

EPHESIANS 4:2 ICB

Don't be a fool
and quickly lose your temper—
be sensible and patient.

PROVERBS 29:11 CEV

Patience is the companion of wisdom.

SAINT AUGUSTINE OF HIPPO

LORD, I NEED PATIENCE AND I NEED IT RIGHT NOW! Have you ever prayed that prayer? Everyone has. Life is hard enough to handle when you're single and taking care of only yourself—but when you have children, patience takes on a whole new meaning!

One definition for patience is: the quality of being patient, as the bearing of provocation, annoyance, misfortune, or pain, without complaint, loss of temper, irritation, or the like.

So what is your patience level when you've given three wake-up calls only to discover, when you hear the sound of the tires of the school bus outside, that your child never got up after all? How about when "little Johnny" asks for the hundredth time why trees are naked in the winter? Or when your children start arguing and punching each other for the tenth time in one day? Do you lose it and then feel guilty for being so impatient?

You're not alone. We all have those days. We feel stretched and anxious about jobs and overloaded schedules and the future. And we take that stress out on our children. Their immaturity is merely our excuse to let out all the steam building up within ourselves. We must remember when all is said and done, that people are the most important thing in our lives, and that includes our children. People are eternal, and our relationships with family and friends are the only things we will take with us into eternity. No matter what is happening around us, we can make the effort to be kind and patient when our kids get on our nerves. They are worth it!

Have you been impatient with your kids lately? Ask for their forgiveness and then ask God to help you treat them with the same kindness that you expect from them.

_____

_____

_____

_____

_____

_____

_____

_____

_____

_____

Peace

Dear Father,

I could use a good dose of "peace on earth." The storms of life are coming against me, and my mind and emotions are being battered by torrents of negative thoughts and circumstances. Fear and anxiety are trying to grip my heart and threaten my sense of well-being.

I run to You, Father. Be to me a refuge where I can find rest for my soul. You are my safe haven until this storm passes, and I trust You to bring me through. Fill our home with Your peace and keep my heart and mind centered on You.

In Jesus' name,
Amen.

[Christ Jesus] is our peace.

EPHESIANS 2:14 GWT

[Jesus said,] "Peace I leave with you; My peace I give to you; not as the world gives do I give to you. Do not let your heart be troubled, nor let it be fearful."

JOHN 14:27 NASB

Let the peace of Christ rule in your hearts, to which indeed you were called in the one body. And be thankful.

COLOSSIANS 3:15 NRSV

You will keep in perfect peace
him whose mind is steadfast,
because he trusts in you.
Trust in the LORD forever,
for the LORD, the LORD, is the Rock eternal.

ISAIAH 26:3–4 NIV

In the day of trouble He will hide me in His shelter;
in the secret place of His tent will He hide me;
He will set me high upon a rock.

PSALM 27:5 AMP

The Rock of Ages and the Prince of Peace are one and the same. Unshakeable peace is found in Him alone.

A SHIP WAS WRECKED IN A FAMOUS STORM, and the only survivor was a little boy who was swept by the waves onto a rock. He sat there all night long until the next morning, when he was spotted and rescued.

"Did you tremble while you were on the rock during the night?" someone later asked him.

"Yes," said the boy. "I trembled all night—but the rock didn't."

Our lives today are filled with stress and danger. Global fears of terrorism and violence can leave us feeling unsettled and worried—especially for our children. Personal stresses, such as a child's illness or unpaid bills, can add up and bring fear of the future. Maybe we aren't literally shipwrecked—but we certainly need a rock to cling to at times.

The good news is that Jesus is our Rock in an uncertain world. David, the psalmist, said of the Lord: "When my heart is faint and overwhelmed, lead me to the mighty, towering Rock of safety" (Psalm 61:2 TLB). Jesus remains stable no matter what storms blow around us. He can be our peace—even in difficult times.

If your heart is "faint and overwhelmed" today, be encouraged with these words: "Be anxious for nothing, but in everything by prayer and supplication with thanksgiving let your requests be made known to God. And the peace of

God, which surpasses all comprehension, will guard your hearts and your minds in Christ Jesus" (Philippians 4:6–7 NASB). Tell God your fears and concerns and let His peace calm you.

What anxieties are threatening your peace today? How can you leave them with the Lord?

_____

_____

_____

_____

_____

_____

_____

_____

_____

_____

_____

_____

Protection

Heavenly Father,

Sometimes I am so concerned about protecting my children and keeping our family safe. The list of things that "could" happen is endless and frightening.

It is impossible for me to protect us by myself, so I look to You—Almighty God. Hide us under the shadow of Your wings and assign angels to keep us safe. Alert us to danger and show us the secure path.

Thank You for constantly watching over us. It is reassuring to know that You are continually listening for our cry. With You we are safe from harm.

In Jesus' name,
Amen.

Those who go to God Most High for safety
will be protected by the Almighty.
I will say to the Lord,
"You are my place of safety and protection.
You are my God and I trust you."

PSALM 91:1–2 NCV

The Lord has heard my cry for help.
The Lord will answer my prayer.

PSALM 6:9 ICB

When the people cry to the Lord for help, he will send
help. He will send someone to save and defend the people.
He will rescue them from those who hurt them.

ISAIAH 19:20 ICB

The Lord says, "Whoever loves me, I will save.
I will protect those who know me.
They will call to me, and I will answer them.
I will be with them in trouble;
I will rescue them and honor them."

PSALM 91:14–15 NCV

When it comes to His children,
God is always on high alert.

ROD COOPER'S FAMILY RAISED PIGS—about a thousand of them a year. In one field they would have two or three hundred little piglets running around. Every day, at four in the morning, as Rod would walk into the field to feed the little oinkers, they'd scatter.

But once, a little pig came up and began to chew on Rod's foot, so he picked it up and began to pet it. Soon the pig wanted down. "No, I'll let you down when I'm ready," Rod said.

At that moment, the piglet let out an ear-piercing squeal. In about two seconds, thirty mama pigs weighing five to six hundred pounds each were headed Rod's way. He put the piglet down and headed for the fence. He barely made it over and looked back to see all the mama pigs walking back and forth and snorting, daring him to come back and mess with one of their own. The piglet had been just one squeal away from rescue.

As a mom, you probably experience the same thing with your children. You can interpret their cries and know when they are just playing and when their "squeals" indicate the need for rescue. And you would do just about anything to protect your children from danger.

How much more do you suppose God wants to protect you, His beloved child? If a mother pig is that sensitive to the cry of her own, how much more sensitive is the Heavenly Father to the cries of His children? When you need protection, like the piglet, you're just one squeal away!

What does your love for your children teach you about God's love for you?

_____

_____

_____

_____

_____

_____

_____

_____

_____

_____

_____

_____

_____

Rest

Heavenly Father,

I am tired and weary. Being a mom is so demanding! Ever since my children were born, I've been on call 24/7, and I never seem to get enough rest.

Will You help me? Give me wisdom regarding my schedule so that I plan wisely and don't set myself up for exhaustion. Help me to set aside a day for rest as You intended, and cause my sleep to be sound and peaceful. Most importantly, help me to discipline myself to spend time with You, for it is in Your presence I find the ultimate rest.

In Jesus' name,
Amen.

"Ask for the old paths, where the good way is,
And walk in it; Then you will find rest for your souls."

JEREMIAH 6:16 NKJV

My soul finds rest in God alone.

PSALM 62:1 NIV

"Six days a week are for your daily duties and
your regular work, but the seventh day is a day of Sabbath
rest before the Lord your God. On that day you are to do
no work of any kind. . . . For in six days the Lord made the
heaven, earth, and sea, and everything in them,
and rested the seventh day; so he blessed the
Sabbath day and set it aside for rest."

EXODUS 20:9–11 TLB

He said, "My Presence will go with you,
and I will give you rest."

EXODUS 33:14 NKJV

My people will abide in a peaceful habitation,
in secure dwellings, and in quiet resting places.

ISAIAH 32:18 NRSV

Take rest; a field that has rested gives a bountiful crop.

OVID

IT SEEMS THAT EVERYONE IN OUR HECTIC SOCIETY TODAY is busy, but moms might be the busiest people of all! First come nightly feedings and changing diapers. Later come soccer practice and parent-teacher conferences. And always there is the ever-present laundry, dishes, and vacuuming. Not to mention, what in the world will you prepare for dinner?

Time-consuming errands and chores can easily steal the enjoyment from our lives. Daily hassles leave us feeling drained and exhausted: "Hurry up, or we'll be late." "No, honey, you shouldn't feed Cheerios to the dog!" "I've only got five minutes to get across town to the Little League game!" These kinds of daily pressures are normal, but when they begin to build up and take over your life, it's time to slow down and get some rest.

Rest is important! Research has shown that the human body needs from six to nine hours of restful sleep each night in order to function properly. When this amount is shortened, the body is robbed of hormones that delay the effects of aging, enhance the immune system, lower cholesterol and blood pressure, rebuild bone and cartilage, elevate mood levels, and increase learning capacity.

Jesus spoke words that are just as real for us today as they were for His disciples two thousand years ago—perhaps even more real considering the society in which we now live: "Come with me by yourselves to a quiet place and get some rest" (Mark 6:31 NIV). He knew that people weren't meant to handle all of the stresses of life without taking a breather now and then.

Take a moment now to be in God's presence, receiving the strength and the rest you need to carry on.

When was the last time you got a good night's sleep?

_____

_____

_____

_____

_____

_____

_____

_____

_____

_____

Self-control

Dear Father,

I feel so defeated. Once again I have given in to my fleshly impulses. Will I ever gain control in this area? Obviously I cannot do this on my own. I need You desperately. Encourage my heart, and let Your grace be multiplied to me.

Even though I feel weak, I stand upon Your promises. Through Christ You have made me more than a conqueror, and I can do all things. Greater are You in me than even my own flesh. I have self-control because it is a fruit of the Spirit. Thank You, Father.

In Jesus' name,
Amen.

No temptation has seized you except what is common to man. And God is faithful; he will not let you be tempted beyond what you can bear. But when you are tempted, he will also provide a way out.

1 Corinthians 10:13 niv

Since [Jesus] himself has now been through suffering and temptation, he knows what it is like when we suffer and are tempted, and he is wonderfully able to help us.

Hebrews 2:18 tlb

[Jesus said,] Watch and pray, that ye enter not into temptation: the spirit indeed is willing, but the flesh is weak.

Matthew 26:41 kjv

If you live according to the sinful nature, you will die; but if by the Spirit you put to death the misdeeds of the body, you will live.

Romans 8:13 niv

The grace of God . . . teaches us to say "No" to ungodliness and worldly passions, and to live self-controlled, upright and godly lives in this present age.

Titus 2:11–12 niv

The secret to self-control is in yielding the control of yourself to the Holy Spirit of God.

SELF-CONTROL. That's a word hardly anyone wants to hear. It means saying no to yourself, and who wants to do that? And it involves discipline—another unpopular word. But in the end, self-control ends up being your friend. It can even save your life. Just ask someone who used to have a weight problem or a drinking problem.

Our fleshly bodies want to live unrestrained. They want to do whatever they want without any consequences. But the truth is: Consequences always follow our actions. So whether we like it or not, we have to say no to ourselves if we want a happy life.

There is a quote that sums it up quite nicely: "Nothing tastes as good as being thin feels." Although this quote specifically refers to eating, it gives us a clue to how we can motivate ourselves to practice discipline. It has a lot to do with our thinking. We can consider discipline a deprivation, or we can tell ourselves the truth. When we discipline ourselves, we give up something of lesser quality for something of higher quality or importance. That is the key. For example, you really want that piece of pie, but you would rather not gain weight so you can wear that great dress to your upcoming party. It is seeing the end result rather than the immediate. It is delayed gratification. In the short term you may suffer, but in the long term you get the payoff.

And when you make a habit of saying no to yourself in certain areas, you form a habit. It gets easier. Down the road, you'll be sitting at your party looking beautiful in your dress. So what if you missed that pie?

In what areas do you need to say no to yourself? What will be your reward if you do?

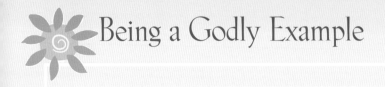

Being a Godly Example

Dear God,

Being a mom can be a daunting responsibility. After all, I am the one my children look to as the example to follow. But I am so aware of my shortcomings and failures, and my children have a front-row seat to every mistake I make!

You would not have given me this assignment unless You knew I could handle it, and I lean heavily on Your grace to help me be what my children need me to be. As You and I walk together daily, may that example influence my children the most.

In the name of Your Son,
Amen.

[Jesus said,] "I have set you an example that
you should do as I have done for you."

JOHN 13:15 NIV

In speech, conduct, love, faith and purity,
show yourself an example of those who believe.

1 TIMOTHY 4:12 NASB

I want you to follow my example and learn from others
who closely follow the example we set for you.

PHILIPPIANS 3:17 CEV

We simply wanted to provide an example of diligence,
hoping it would prove contagious.

2 THESSALONIANS 3:9 MSG

God was merciful to me in order that Christ Jesus might
show his full patience in dealing with me, the worst of
sinners, as an example for all those who would later believe
in him and receive eternal life.

1 TIMOTHY 1:16 GNT

*Nothing is more contagious than example,
and no man does any exceeding good or exceeding ill
but it spawns new deeds of the same kind.*

FRANÇOIS, DUC DE LA ROCHEFOUCAULD

AS A MOM, IT'S IMPORTANT TO REALIZE that everything you do is being observed by "little eyes." As daunting as that may sound, it is really a good thing. By your example, your children can learn how to live a godly life before they venture out on their own. What a blessing for them, and what a privilege for you. You get to profoundly affect them for good.

Now, you might be thinking, *But I'm not a good influencer. I've made too many mistakes!* But in reality, if you are seeking the Lord with all your heart and trying to follow Him the best you can, He can even use your mistakes to benefit your child. Your life becomes an object lesson for your children that shows them how to, or how not to, respond to situations. As they see you mess up but then receive forgiveness from God, they will realize that they, too, can be forgiven. When they watch you dust yourself off and get back up, they will learn tenacity and the principle of never giving up! As they see you repenting before God and apologizing to others when you have sinned, they will be taught to admit and deal with their own sin.

What a great way to instill values in your children! It was all God's idea. And since He created the process, He can give you the wisdom to take full advantage of the opportunity—a chance for you to partner with God in one of the most important tasks ever assigned—to show your children the way to follow Him. It is the greatest gift you could ever give them!

Name one good thing your children have learned by watching your life.

_____

_____

_____

_____

_____

_____

_____

_____

_____

_____

_____

_____

_____

_____

Believing the Best

Dear Lord,

I'm finding it difficult to see my children in a positive light today. We have been over and over the same issues, yet they continue to disobey. They sense my frustration and disapproval, and that only perpetuates the problem.

Lord, help me to believe the best of my children instead of expecting the worst. Enable me to separate their behavior from who they are and to discipline consistently and fairly. I want to love them unconditionally like You love me and to communicate it in such a way that they feel cherished and valuable.

In Jesus' name,
Amen.

"Man looks at the outward appearance,
but the Lord looks at the heart."

1 Samuel 16:7 nkjv

[Jesus said,] "Treat others just as you
want to be treated."

Luke 6:31 cev

[Jesus said,] "My command is this:
Love each other as I have loved you."

John 15:12 niv

Above all, maintain constant love for one another,
for love covers a multitude of sins.

1 Peter 4:8 nrsv

Accept one another, just as Christ also accepted us
to the glory of God.

Romans 15:7 nasb

*What parents believe about their children often becomes a self-
fulfilling prophecy. Believe the best!*

DO YOU BELIEVE THE BEST OF YOUR CHILDREN? Sometimes it's hard—especially when you see the crayon marks all over the wall or when your teenager just wrecked the car. But it is crucial for you to do so.

Everyone makes mistakes, and we all need discipline. But we also need to know that someone thinks we are okay even when we mess up. That is what love does. First Corinthians 13:7 TLB says, "If you love someone you will be loyal to him no matter what the cost. You will always believe in him, always expect the best of him. . . ."

As a parent, this is one of the most difficult things to do. We need to discipline, though somehow we must stress that the action is bad but the child isn't. This helps a child maintain a healthy self-esteem. He can be held accountable for his wrongdoing, but he knows that he is a child deeply loved and cherished by you. Your belief in him lets him know that God loves him just the way he is. Sometimes this is especially hard to do if your parents didn't believe in you. You may need to ask God to heal that "worth" issue in your own heart so that you can give that unconditional acceptance to your child.

So, the next time your child gets into trouble, stop and think for a moment. Instead of believing the worst—this child will never do the right thing; this child is hopeless—ask God to show you your child through His eyes. You may see something totally amazing!

List five good qualities your child (or children) exhibit.

Children's Future

Heavenly Father,

What a privilege it is to be the mother of such amazing children! I marvel when I consider how precious and unique they are, Your handiwork indeed.

It is also a tremendous responsibility when I realize that You have ordained my children to be on earth at this particular time in history, assigning to each a specific task. Help me to recognize the gifts and talents with which You have equipped my children, and show me how to nurture those abilities so that they can fulfill their destiny for Your glory.

In Jesus' name,
Amen.

"I know the plans I have for you," declares the LORD, "plans to prosper you and not to harm you, plans to give you hope and a future."

JEREMIAH 29:11 NIV

The plans of the LORD stand firm forever,
the purposes of his heart through all generations.

PSALM 33:11 NIV

The LORD will fulfill his purpose for me;
your love, O LORD, endures forever—
do not abandon the works of your hands.

PSALM 138:8 NIV

I have filled you with the Spirit of God, with skill,
ability and knowledge in all kinds of crafts.

EXODUS 31:3 NIV

God gives us many kinds of special abilities, but it is the same Holy Spirit who is the source of them all.

1 CORINTHIANS 12:4 TLB

Helping a child discover his or her destiny is like opening a beautifully wrapped package to discover the treasure inside.

❋

EXPERTS NOW SAY THAT YOU CAN ACTUALLY GET CLUES to the talents and abilities in children by watching them play. Do any of your children love to organize things? Or have a special interest in animals and the outdoors? You never know—one may become a professional organizer someday. Another might become a famous wildlife biologist. It's important to be alert to see the direction in which your children may lean.

We all want our children to be successful, but sometimes we want something for them that doesn't fit with their giftings. Watch your children and encourage them in the things that spark their interest. Encouragement means speaking your words of affirmation as well as providing the opportunities for them to test the waters. If one child likes to draw, why not let that one take a painting class. If it turns out that this child isn't inclined to this pursuit, it wasn't wasted time. Children enjoy the process of finding out who they are and will have the courage to try other new things as they see your support.

And a word of warning. We sometimes have in our minds what we would like our children to become. We may want one to be a doctor or a minister because Grandpa so-and-so was of that vocation, and it is a family tradition. But the most important question you can ask yourself is this: What does God want my children to be? Pray that the Lord will give you wisdom to see the special abilities He has placed in them.

Why not spend a little time watching your child play today?

List some of the interests of your children.

_____

_____

_____

_____

_____

_____

_____

_____

_____

_____

_____

_____

_____

Children's Obedience

Heavenly Father,

I need Your assistance in getting my children to obey. To begin with, help me to be fair and to set standards according to Your Word. Then help me express my love in such a way that my children feel it.

Next, I pray that You will create in my children's hearts the desire to obey. Our home will be more pleasant, but You also promise that it will go well with them and that they will be blessed with longevity. May their obedience to me lead to a life of obedience to You.

In Jesus' name,
Amen.

Train children in the right way,
and when old, they will not stray.

PROVERBS 22:6 NRSV

Children, obey your parents in the Lord, for this is right.
"Honor your father and mother"—this is the first
commandment with a promise: "so that it may be well
with you and you may live long on the earth."
And, fathers, do not provoke your children to anger,
but bring them up in the discipline and
instruction of the Lord.

EPHESIANS 6:1–4 NRSV

The person who loves his children is
careful to correct them.

PROVERBS 13:24 ICB

[The Lord says,] "I have given you my power and my
teachings to be yours forever, and from now on you are to
obey me and teach your children and your descendants to
obey me for all time to come."

ISAIAH 59:21 GNT

To correct a child is the purest form of a parent's love.

ONE OF THE GREAT CHALLENGES OF MOTHERHOOD is teaching your child the value of obedience. Just when you think you have this area mastered, your child goes through another stage of exerting his or her independence, and it can feel as if you're starting all over again.

How can you effectively instill obedience in your children without squelching their independence and creativity? The best place to start is in prayer. Ask God for the wisdom to know when to be unyielding and consistent in your discipline and when you may be able to cut your child some slack. Then ask for the strength and perseverance to carry through on the wisdom He gives.

Your requirements of obedience should always be based on the loving trust relationship between you and your child, and this relationship must be built over time. Take every opportunity to get to know your children individually and to enjoy the good things they do. When they are confident of getting this positive attention from you, they'll be much less likely to behave badly in order to get your attention. As much as is possible and at a level they can understand, take the time to explain why you ask them to do or not do certain things. Although it may seem like a long process at times, the time and attention you pour into your child's life will translate into great dividends later on.

When your children experience firsthand the benefits of obeying you, their earthly parent, they'll be more open to obeying their Heavenly Father and to following the Holy Spirit's leading in their lives.

In what ways can you build upon the trust relationship between you and your child?

Heavenly Father,

There are many important things I desire for my children, but the most crucial of all is their salvation. Give me wisdom on ways to whet their appetites for Christ, and help me to set an appealing example before them. Surround my children with godly friends to share the Good News in a way they can grasp, and soften their hearts that they may be receptive.

I pray that the truth will dawn on my children and that they will make Jesus the Lord of their lives. Then, together, we will spend eternity worshiping You.

In Jesus' name,
Amen.

"Believe in the Lord Jesus, and you will be saved—
you and your household."

Acts 16:31 niv

[Jesus said,] "You are light for the world. . . .
No one lights a lamp and puts it under a basket.
Instead, everyone who lights a lamp puts it on a lamp
stand. Then its light shines on everyone in the house."

Matthew 5:14–15 gwt

[Jesus said,] "Plead with the Lord of the harvest to send
out more laborers to help you."

Luke 10:2 tlb

He wants not only us but everyone saved . . .
to know the truth.

1 Timothy 2:4 msg

Always remember these commands I give you today.
Teach them to your children. Talk about them when you
sit at home and walk along the road. Talk about them
when you lie down and when you get up.

Deuteronomy 6:6–7 icb

You are "Jesus with skin on" for your children.
Represent Him well.

SUSANNA WESLEY ONCE SAID THAT HER GOAL WAS to "save her children's souls." Raised in a Christian home, she valued the importance of a personal relationship with God. She made it a priority to instruct her own children in the faith. She started a daily school for them for this very purpose. Although other academics were studied, God's Word was preeminent.

She was often alone in this task of imparting spiritual truth to her children due to her husband's many problems. But her tireless efforts paid off. John, one of her sons, became a renowned preacher who founded the organization that would become the Methodist church. Another son, Charles, wrote hundreds of hymns such as "O For a Thousand Tongues to Sing" and "Hark the Herald Angels Sing." Both became men of faith who affected their generation for Christ.

Susanna Wesley realized that the best gift she could give her children was to introduce them to a loving God. And that is the best gift you can give your children.

You may not feel up to the task, but here are a few suggestions that may help:

- Take your children to a Bible-believing church regularly.
- Take a class on sharing your faith so that you can talk to them about the Lord.

- Pray that God will send others to share the gospel with your kids.
- Encourage your children to participate in Christian activities like camp, youth group, or a Christian club.
- Read the Bible with your kids and pray with them. Start a prayer journal where you record God's answers to prayers.

As you do these things, you give God an open door to work in your children's lives.

Do your children have a personal relationship with Christ? If not, what steps will you take so that they have the opportunity to know Him?

Commitment

Father God,

I want my children to stick to their commitments, and I know that starts with me. Help me to set a good example by always being a person of my word. Give me the discipline to follow through on my promises, no matter what the cost, and give me wisdom to help my children do the same.

This type of commitment is necessary for us to be good witnesses and to please You. When I meet You face-to-face, I want You to be able to say, "Well done. You were committed to the end."

In Jesus' name,
Amen.

Lord, who may enter your Temple?
Who may worship on Zion, your sacred hill?
Those who obey God in everything
and always do what is right,
whose words are true and sincere . . .
They always do what they promise,
no matter how much it may cost.

Psalm 15:1–2, 4 gnt

If you make a promise to God,
don't be slow to keep it. . . .
It is better not to promise anything than
to promise something and not do it.

Ecclesiastes 5:4–5 ncv

Fear God. Worship him in total commitment.

Joshua 24:14 msg

God delights in those who keep their promises.

Proverbs 12:22 tlb

*Commitment in children begins by their parents
being committed to them.*

✳

SUSIE WAS SO EXCITED. Her mom had promised her that she would take her swimming on Saturday. All week long, Susie anticipated the sun and fun at the community pool. But when Saturday came, her mom had a few errands to run. They never made it to the pool.

Unfortunately, this plays out repeatedly in some families. But what is a family if it is not a community of people who dare to make a promise and who care enough to keep it, no matter what comes their way? A family is not just two or more people related by blood who happen to live under one roof. It is a group of people who honor each other and keep their words.

Granted, sometimes things happen out of our control that prevent us from keeping a commitment. But in those times, we need to explain the situation to our children and others and come up with a different solution.

As a mom, you want to be there for your kids, but sometimes it's tough to keep those commitments. It's in those times of difficulty that you can rely on God's Spirit to help you. Just as "He who promised is faithful" (Hebrews 10:23 NIV), God can help you keep your promises to your husband and children. He will help you stick to the tasks before you, even when you want to give up. And His rewards are great!

As you continue to be faithful to your loved ones, your kids will learn what it really means to make and keep a commitment. Your family will become a shining example of God's love and faithfulness in a chaotic world that rarely keeps its promises.

What specific commitments have you made to your children recently? How do you intend to keep those commitments?

Conflict at Home

Dear God,

Home is supposed to be a refuge, but right now, conflict is brewing. I don't want us to live in a war zone, but in a haven of love and support.

Father, help us with this. Teach us how to resolve our conflicts, to put each other first, and to have the kind of relationships that You intended. Show us how we can work together rather than against one another so that we all win. Fill our home with Your peace and unity, for it is there that You can shower Your blessings.

In Jesus' name,
Amen.

Hate starts quarrels,
but love covers every wrong.

<small>Proverbs 10:12 gwt</small>

A gentle answer will calm a person's anger,
but an unkind answer will cause more anger.

<small>Proverbs 15:1 ncv</small>

Starting a quarrel is like a leak in a dam.
So stop the quarrel before a fight breaks out.

<small>Proverbs 17:14 icb</small>

How very good and pleasant it is
when kindred live together in unity! . . .
For there the Lord ordained his blessing,
life forevermore.

<small>Psalm 133:1, 3 nrsv</small>

Don't be quick to fly off the handle.
Anger boomerangs. You can spot a fool by the lumps on
his head.

<small>Ecclesiastes 7:9 msg</small>

*Life is tough. Home is the one place we should find emotional
safety, comfort, support, and love.*

A MARRIED COUPLE had a quarrel and ended up giving each other the silent treatment. A week into their mute argument, the man realized that he needed his wife's help. In order to catch a flight to Chicago for a business meeting, he had to get up at 5 a.m.

Not wanting to be the first to break the silence, he wrote on a piece of paper, "Please wake me at 5 a.m."

The next morning, the man woke up only to discover that his wife was already out of bed, it was 9 a.m., and his flight had long since departed. He was about to find his wife and demand an explanation for her failings when he noticed a piece of paper by the bed.

He read, "It's 5 a.m. Wake up."

Conflict within a marriage relationship or a family is never fun—but when it is left unresolved, it can be detrimental to everyone. Children are hit especially hard when fights erupt or when the silent treatment eats away at the atmosphere in a home. Studies have shown that family conflicts cause much greater amounts of stress in a child's life than failing at schoolwork, conflict with peers, or even living in poverty.

If you are experiencing conflict with your spouse or another family member, remember that silence is not the answer. Communication is the key to resolving differences, and learning good communication skills takes time and effort. Sometimes an outside counselor, such as a pastor or professional therapist, can be a great resource to help you sort through your issues. But even more important, you always have that Wonderful Counselor, the Holy Spirit, available to help. When you invite Him to be the center of your family, He will make your home into a place of love, joy, and peace.

How do you usually resolve conflicts?

_____

_____

_____

_____

_____

_____

_____

_____

_____

_____

_____

Disciplining

Heavenly Father,

When it comes to disciplining my children, I need Your input and direction. It's so hard for me to get it right. My tendency is to either let things go or to punish too harshly. It all takes so much energy!

Father, teach me to discipline the way that You do—lovingly, consistently, and fairly. Help me not to lose my temper or say things I will regret. Your correction may hurt at the time, but it bears wonderful fruit. May the same be said of the discipline in our home.

In Jesus' name,
Amen.

The corrections of discipline
are the way to life.

PROVERBS 6:23 NIV

A wise child loves discipline,
but a scoffer does not listen to rebuke.

PROVERBS 13:1 NRSV

Discipline your children while there is hope;
do not set your heart on their destruction.

PROVERBS 19:18 NRSV

Discipline your children, and they will give you rest;
they will give delight to your heart.

PROVERBS 29:17 NRSV

My son,
listen to your father's discipline,
and do not neglect your mother's teachings,
because discipline and teachings
are a graceful garland on your head.

PROVERBS 1:8–9 GWT

*Let thy child's first lesson be obedience,
and the second will be what thou wilt.*

BENJAMIN FRANKLIN

FIVE-YEAR-OLD BARBARA HAD DISOBEYED HER MOTHER and had been sent to her room. After a few minutes, her mom went in to talk with her about what she had done. Teary-eyed, she asked, "Why do we do wrong things, Mommy?"

"Well," her mom replied, "sometimes the devil tells us to do something wrong, and we listen to him. We need to listen to God instead."

To which Barbara sobbed, "But God doesn't talk loud enough!"

Disciplining a child may be one of the most difficult and unpleasant things you may need to do as a mom—but it is one of the most important. Just as Barbara needed to learn to hear God's voice better, your children, too, need you to point them in the right direction, to help them hear God's voice and be willing to obey.

The Bible has much to say about disciplining your children. The Old Testament proverbs admonish: "He who spares the rod hates his son, but he who loves him is careful to discipline him" (Proverbs 13:24 NIV); "Train up a child in the way he should go, and when he is old he will not depart from it" (Proverbs 22:6 NKJV). The New Testament also encourages parents: "Bring [your children] up with the discipline and instruction approved by the Lord" (Ephesians 6:4 NLT [96]).

Although discipline isn't "fun" at the time, it will lead your children into a happier and more stable, productive life—the life that God wants them to live. It will help them to better hear God's voice in the future and be willing to obey, which will reap benefits far beyond what they can currently imagine. They will thank you for it later!

How can you turn discipline into a positive experience for both you and your child?

_____

_____

_____

_____

_____

_____

_____

_____

_____

_____

_____

Father in Heaven,

This whole idea of living by faith—believing in things I cannot see—is not always easy. My tendency is to go solely by what my senses and experience tell me, but I know they can be unreliable. You and Your Word, on the other hand, are utterly trustworthy.

Lead me to Your promises that address my concerns; then help me to rest in them. What a blessing it is to not be restricted to this natural world. By faith, all things become possible as You watch over Your Word to perform it.

In Jesus' name,
Amen.

Fight the good fight of faith.

1 Timothy 6:12 ncv

Remember those who led you,
who spoke the word of God to you; and considering the
result of their conduct, imitate their faith.

Hebrews 13:7 nasb

Faith means being sure of the things we hope for and
knowing that something is real even if we do not see it.

Hebrews 11:1 ncv

Have faith in God! If you have faith in God and don't
doubt, you can tell this mountain to get up and jump into
the sea, and it will. Everything you ask for in prayer will be
yours, if you only have faith.

Mark 11:22–24 cev

[Abraham's] faith did not leave him, and he did not doubt
God's promise; his faith filled him with power, and he gave
praise to God. He was absolutely sure that God would be
able to do what he had promised.

Romans 4:20–21 gnt

*Faith is to believe what we do not see;
and the reward of this faith is to see what we believe.*

Saint Augustine

RAISING CHILDREN REQUIRES A GREAT DEAL OF FAITH. You need faith to believe God will guide you in your parenting as you attempt to teach your children those things they most need to know in life. Faith is required in order to trust God to take care of your family's daily needs. And an even greater amount of faith is required of you to trust God to take care of your children when they venture outside the boundaries of your watchful care.

As you talk with God today, ask Him for the faith you will need to face the challenges of the day with strength and wisdom. Ask Him to provide for your daily needs; then trust Him to do it. And when your children are away from you, ask God for His protection and guidance to surround them and lead their steps.

Choosing to parent by faith is not taking the easy road. In fact, our natural instinct is to want to handle things on our own, especially when it comes to our children. But by relying on God rather than on your own abilities, you'll save yourself a great deal of stress and anxiety and will provide a much richer child-hood for your children, allowing them the freedom to develop into the people God wants them to be. Best of all, they will learn from your example how to trust in and rely upon their loving Heavenly Father, a legacy of faith that will be a great blessing to them throughout their lives.

In what areas of your parenting could you exercise more faith?

Faithfulness

Dear Father,

One of the things I most appreciate about You is that no matter what, You are faithful. I want my children to be able to say the same about me because it will help them feel safe and secure.

When I would rather take the path of least resistance, give me the grace to do the right thing, to be faithful even in the smallest areas. And I ask You to give my children a desire to be faithful as well, for it yields a life of great favor and blessing from You.

In Jesus' name,
Amen.

Know that the Lord has set apart the faithful for himself;
the Lord hears when I call to him.

Psalm 4:3 nrsv

The faithful will abound with blessings,
but one who is in a hurry to be rich will not go
unpunished.

Proverbs 28:20 nrsv

Do not let loyalty and faithfulness forsake you;
bind them around your neck,
write them on the tablet of your heart.
So you will find favor and good repute
in the sight of God and of people.

Proverbs 3:3–4 nrsv

The Lord loves the just
and will not forsake his faithful ones.
They will be protected forever.

Psalm 37:28 niv

Mine eyes shall be upon the faithful of the land.

Psalm 101:6 kjv

Faithfulness in little things is a big thing.

Saint John Chrysostom

MOST ARE FAMILIAR WITH THE PHRASE, A "FAITHFUL FRIEND." It reminds us of someone who is true and loyal. But there is another aspect of faithfulness. It involves doing what is required day in and day out when the reward is not necessarily in sight. This aspect is not as prevalent in people's lives today.

But it hasn't always been so. Consider how people used to view employment. Just a generation ago, people realized that a lifetime of being faithful paid off in a secure retirement. Back then, it was common knowledge that the people who proved themselves got the raises and the promotions. Faithfulness was rewarded.

But in our instant society, we no longer reward faithfulness. Everyone wants to get ahead quickly without the hard work. As unpopular as it may seem in our culture, God still values and rewards faithfulness. Throughout His Word, He stresses its importance and promises its rewards.

Faithfulness is also closely associated with trustworthiness. If someone is trustworthy, they are dependable and reliable—they can be trusted. This is the type of person that people want as their friend and whom they want to hire. Not only will others view them as an asset, but God will also be pleased.

Therefore it's important to train your children to be

faithful. When you see them doing their chores day by day with a good attitude, tell them you're pleased. If they stick with their studies even when they're having a hard time understanding, reward them. Let them know that their faithfulness has not gone unnoticed. Not only will God be pleased, but they will have the satisfaction of knowing they are doing what is right.

What are some ways you can teach your children to be faithful?

_____

_____

_____

_____

_____

_____

_____

_____

_____

_____

Finances

Heavenly Father,

Money matters are so complicated, and it's hard to find the balance, especially when it comes to my children. I want to bless them with the desires of their hearts, but I also want to instill a grateful attitude.

Teach us to view money rightly, to manage it wisely, and to never allow it to control us. As we put You first, I trust You to provide the finances we need, plus abundance, so we can bless others. Help us to never be greedy or stingy but to always be thankful for Your provision.

In Jesus' name,
Amen.

My God will richly fill your every need in a glorious way
through Christ Jesus.

Philippians 4:19 GWT

"Don't worry and ask yourselves, 'Will we have anything
to eat? Will we have anything to drink? Will we have any
clothes to wear?' Only people who don't know God are
always worrying about such things. Your Father in heaven
knows that you need all of these. But more than anything
else, put God's work first and do what he wants.
Then the other things will be yours as well."

Matthew 6:31–33 CEV

I have been young, and now am old; yet have I not seen
the righteous forsaken, nor his seed begging bread.

Psalm 37:25 KJV

[Jesus said,] "Your Father knows the things you need before
you ask him. So when you pray, you should pray like this:
'Our Father in heaven, . . .
Give us the food we need for each day.'"

Matthew 6:8–9, 11 ICB

*God has unlimited resources at His disposal, and He delights
in making them available to His children.*

WE ALL HAVE OUR STRUGGLES WITH FINANCES. In our consumer-driven society, any amount of income can seem like it's never quite enough—particularly when it comes to raising children. We want to provide the very best for our kids, which often translates into money to pay for the latest in educational toys, the best schools, extracurricular activities, clothes, shoes, dentist bills, savings for college—the list goes on. We want our children to have the very best in life, yet we don't want to "spoil" them. Walking this line can become a source of great strife among families, particularly when the money is simply not there.

What does the Bible have to say about our finances? First, it warns us: "No one can serve two masters. . . . You cannot serve both God and Money" (Matthew 6:24 NIV). Next, it assures us that God will take care of our needs. Matthew 6:26 NIV says, "Look at the birds of the air; they do not sow or reap or store away in barns, and yet your heavenly Father feeds them. Are you not much more valuable than they?" Finally, it admonishes us to "seek first [God's] kingdom and his righteousness, and all these things will be given to you as well" (Matthew 6:33 NIV).

If we are seeking after God's best for our children, we

have no need for worry. He knows even better than we do exactly what our children need, and He will be faithful to provide it at just the right time. We can trust Him in this.

List some things you'd like to be financially able to provide for your children. In your prayer time, ask God to provide those things that line up with His best for them and to bring your desires for them into agreement with His.

_____

_____

_____

_____

_____

_____

_____

_____

_____

_____

Forgiving My Child

Heavenly Father,

Before I had children, I had no idea I would have to practice forgiving them as often as I do! Sometimes I get so angry, and that only compounds the problem. It's hard not to take their offenses personally.

I know how important forgiveness is, but I need Your help. Once I decide to forgive, help me to manage my emotions well so that I can truly restore the relationship between my children and me. I want to afford them the same blessing that You offer me every time I blow it.

In Jesus' name,
Amen.

"Our Father in heaven, . . . forgive us our sins,
just as we have forgiven those who have sinned against us.
. . . Your heavenly Father will forgive you if you forgive
those who sin against you; but if you refuse to forgive
them, he will not forgive you."

Matthew 6:9,12,14–15 tlb

Be gentle with one another, sensitive. Forgive one another
as quickly and thoroughly as God in Christ forgave you.

Ephesians 4:32 msg

Peter came up to the Lord and asked, "How many times
should I forgive someone who does something wrong to
me? Is seven times enough?" Jesus answered: "Not just
seven times, but seventy-seven times!"

Matthew 18:21–22 cev

If anyone has caused grief . . . you ought to forgive
and comfort him, so that he will not be overwhelmed
by excessive sorrow. I urge you, therefore, to reaffirm
your love for him.

2 Corinthians 2:1, 7–8 niv

*Forgiveness is a funny thing—
it warms the heart and cools the sting.*

William Arthur Ward

WHEN YOUR CHILD DOES SOMETHING THAT HURTS OR OFFENDS YOU, it's important that you extend forgiveness to him or her in the same way God forgives us when we sin against Him. Your child needs to understand what forgiveness is—and what it is not.

Being forgiven doesn't mean we don't face the consequences of our actions. You can forgive your children without excusing them from punishment for their behavior. Just be sure that the punishment is based on your love and concern for your child's future well-being rather than on your own feelings of anger.

Forgiveness does mean that the relationship between you and your child is completely restored—that the incident will no longer create any kind of barrier between you or affect your feelings toward your child in any way. Psalm 103:12 NIV describes God's forgiveness of us in this way: "As far as the east is from the west, so far has he removed our transgressions from us." Similarly, Jeremiah 31:34 NIV says, "I will forgive their wickedness and will remember their sins no more." Once words of forgiveness have been spoken, do your best to forget the incident. Don't say or do things that cause your children to relive their mistakes or to feel they are being identified by their bad behavior.

Offering genuine, Christlike forgiveness to your children will strengthen your relationship with them and will let them know they can trust you to act justly. Even more importantly, it will help them to understand the depth of God's love and forgiveness for them.

Are there areas of unforgiveness in your relationships with any of your children? If so, what steps can you take to right the situation?

Friendship

Heavenly Father,

Thank You for the wonderful friends You have given me. Since having children, though, it has become increasingly difficult to spend quality time with these special people. Life mostly revolves around my children these days.

Help me find ways to stay connected with my friends from the past and to make time for the friends I have through my current activities. In addition, lead me to new friends with kindred hearts. In each friendship, may we be a mutual encouragement to each other and help each other grow in our individual walks with You.

In Jesus' name,
Amen.

A friend loves you all the time.

PROVERBS 17:17 ICB

A friendly discussion is as stimulating as the sparks
that fly when iron strikes iron.

PROVERBS 27:17 TLB

The righteous person is a guide to his friend,
but the path of the wicked leads them astray.

PROVERBS 12:26 GNT

[Jesus said,] "No one has greater love than this,
to lay down one's life for one's friends."

JOHN 15:13 NRSV

Some friends play at friendship
but a true friend sticks closer than one's nearest kin.

PROVERBS 18:24 NRSV

I am a friend to everyone who fears you.
I am a friend to anyone who follows your orders.

PSALM 119:63 ICB

A friend is a person with whom I may think aloud.

RALPH WALDO EMERSON

WHERE DO YOUR FRIENDSHIPS FALL ON YOUR LIST OF PRIORITIES? Your friendships can be an immeasurable source of joy, strength, and comfort to you as you travel through the adventures of motherhood.

Perhaps you have a friend, or several friends, in whom you can confide—friends who understand the ups and downs of motherhood and are there for you with a listening ear and an open heart. If so, treasure these friendships. Even though your life is busy, make sure you invest time into these friendships and that you let these friends know how much you appreciate and value them. Be there to support them when they are in need of your friendship.

Maybe you feel you're too busy with work or all your children's activities to keep up with friendships. But don't allow a busy schedule to rob you of the immense blessings friendship can bring to your life. Find ways to seek out friendships while fulfilling your daily duties. When you're at your child's ball game or practice, why not strike up a conversation with another mom? You just may find someone with whom you have a great deal in common. Getting to know the parents of your children's friends is a great way to be involved in your children's lives and may very well be a source of blossoming friendships for you as well.

You never know where you may find a kindred spirit, but they are readily available if you'll seek them out, and the friendships you'll develop will be well worth the time and effort you'll put into them.

List some things you could do to build on the friendships you have or to develop new friendships.

_____

_____

_____

_____

_____

_____

_____

_____

_____

_____

_____

_____

_____

Guilt

Heavenly Father,

Guilt is weighing heavily on me. It is as though my failures are etched permanently on my mind, and I have become stuck. I need Your help to break this unhealthy mindset.

The truth is, You forgave me as soon as I confessed these errors, and then You erased them from Your memory. Now I ask You to help me erase them from my mind as well. As I focus on the cleansing blood of Jesus and Your forgiveness, comfort me and reassure me of Your love so I can be free of this guilt.

In Jesus' name,
Amen.

I confessed my sins to you.
I didn't hide my guilt.
I said, "I will confess my sins to the Lord."
And you forgave my guilt.

PSALM 32:5 ICB

[The Lord says,]
I alone am the one who is going to wipe away
your rebellious actions
for my own sake.
I will not remember your sins [anymore.]

ISAIAH 43:25 GWT

Our God, you bless everyone
whose sins you forgive
and wipe away.
You bless them by saying,
"You told me your sins,
without trying to hide them,
and now I forgive you."

PSALM 32:1–2 CEV

*The blood of Jesus erases once and for all
the stain of guilt.*

 ONE DAY POLLY AND HER GRANDDAUGHTER, SUSAN, WERE WATCHING A PLANE skywrite letters across the sky. The little girl was puzzled when the words began disappearing, but then she suddenly piped up: "Maybe Jesus has an eraser!"

Susan's innocent wisdom contains an important truth. Just as the skywriting disappears from the clouds, Jesus wipes away all the sins we so bitterly regret committing. All we have to do is ask.

No mom is ever perfect. It's easy to become angry or frustrated and do or say things that we don't mean. But the Bible tells us that our sins are forgiven when we confess them to the Lord: "If we confess our sins, He is faithful and just to forgive us our sins and to cleanse us from all unrighteousness" (1 John 1:9 NKJV). God's Word also informs us that "there is therefore now no condemnation to those who are in Christ Jesus" (Romans 8:1 NKJV). If you are feeling guilty or ashamed today over sins that you have already confessed to the Lord, those feelings don't come from God. Once He has forgiven you and cleansed you from that sin, He will never bring it up again. Psalm 103:12 NASB confirms this: "As far as the east is from the west, so far has He removed our transgressions from us."

No matter how much we mature as Christians, memories of our own failures, especially our failures as a parent, may still try to rise up and haunt us. But with God's forgiveness, they will fade away. Jesus does have an eraser.

What things have you done wrong as a parent?
What things have you done right?

_____

_____

_____

_____

_____

_____

_____

_____

_____

_____

_____

_____

_____

_____

_____

Healing of My Child

Father in Heaven,

I come to You on behalf of my child who is sick. Thank You for being a compassionate Father who cares about every detail of our lives.

You said in Your Word that if a child were to ask his earthly father for a fish, he would not give him a snake. In the same way, You will give good to those who ask You. So I ask You to give my child healing today. Thank You for Your supernatural touch.

In Jesus' name,
Amen.

Jesus rebuked the unclean spirit, and healed the child,
and delivered him again to his father.

LUKE 9:42 KJV

Abraham prayed to God. And God healed Abimelech,
his wife and his servant girls.

GENESIS 20:17 ICB

Everyone who believes me will be able to do wonderful
things. By using my name they will . . . heal sick people by
placing their hands on them.

MARK 16:17–18 CEV

Are any among you sick? They should call for the elders of
the church and have them pray over them, anointing them
with oil in the name of the Lord. The prayer of faith will
save the sick, and the Lord will raise them up.

JAMES 5:14–15 NRSV

[Christ's] wounds have healed you.

1 PETER 2:24 GWT

The power of Jesus brings healing and peace to
spirit, soul, and body.

✳

WHEN THIRTEEN-YEAR-OLD HEATHER FIRST COMPLAINED of discomfort on her right side, her mom wasn't too concerned. But when, several days later, she was writhing and crying in pain, it was obvious something was terribly wrong. The doctor confirmed what Heather's mom already suspected: appendicitis. He wrote it in big, bold letters across her chart.

On the way to the hospital, Heather was in agony, but her mom began to pray a prayer of healing over her body. Heather practically had to be carried into the emergency room, but her mom still kept praying. Even when the blood tests and ultrasound confirmed that her appendix was extremely inflamed, Heather's mother continued to ask for a miracle.

And then, something began to happen; Heather suddenly began to feel better. Soon the pain was completely gone. And another ultrasound confirmed it; her appendix was completely normal.

God loves to heal His children. Even though it can be frightening for parents when a child is sick, it is important to remember that Jesus is the Great Physician—and that He loves little children. He once said: "Let the children come to me. Don't stop them! For the Kingdom of Heaven belongs to those who are like these [children]" (Matthew 19:14 NLT).

If your child is sick today, bring him or her to the Heavenly Father. Ask Him to touch your child's body and bring strength and relief from pain. God loves your child even more than you do, and He longs to bring comfort and healing where it is needed the most.

From what does your child need healing the most?

_____

_____

_____

_____

_____

_____

_____

_____

_____

_____

_____

_____

Humility

Father God,

You hate pride, so I don't want it to have any part in me. I want to be humble like Jesus.

Having the proper attitude about myself is tricky, though. It is so easy to think too highly of myself in one area while in another I put myself down. Help me to see myself the way that You do. Any of my good attributes and accomplishments are a result of You, and the blood of Jesus makes up for my shortcomings. Help me to find the balance, so I can walk in true humility.

In Jesus' name,
Amen.

Are there any of you who are wise and understanding?
You are to prove it by your good life, by your good deeds
performed with humility and wisdom.

JAMES 3:13 GNT

You save humble people,
but you bring down a conceited look.

PSALM 18:27 GWT

I [the Lord] will renew the spirit of those who are humble.

ISAIAH 57:15 GWT

Humility comes before honor.

PROVERBS 15:33 GWT

The reward for humility and fear of the LORD
is riches and honor and life.

PROVERBS 22:4 NRSV

Pride ends in a fall, while humility brings honor.

PROVERBS 29:23 TLB

*Humility is recognizing that everything we have and every-
thing we are comes from God.*

❋

 WHEN WE THINK OF HUMILITY, OFTEN WE THINK OF A PERSON WHO IS a doormat and never speaks his or her mind. The Bible paints a totally different picture. Jesus exhibited humility, yet He drove the money changers out of the temple and exposed the hypocrisy of the Pharisees. (Matthew 21:12–13; 22:15–22.)

Through Jesus' example, we can see that a humble person accepts his shortcomings and doesn't need to belittle himself over them. He also accepts his talents but doesn't gloat over them. He recognizes that everything he has is a gift from God, so he knows he can take no credit. He is not shy about using all the abilities God has given him, because he is submitted to God and knows that God is pleased when he lives out what God made him to be. Jesus was a truly humble individual but was powerful. His life angered many. People often wondered, *Who does He think He is?* He knew who He was—that was the point! Some people just didn't like it. He could've tried to appease them and cover up who He was, but that would not have been humility. That would have been people-pleasing!

Humility also means you'll never think more of yourself than you should. You're not better than anyone else, and you're not below anyone else except God. He is preeminent, and you're not. You show no greater humility than when you confess to God your need for His intervention in your life. When you look to Him to meet your needs, when you trust Him, you are allowing Him to be who He is—God—and you are being who you are—the one who needs Him.

Name some areas in your life where you need to show humility. Ask God to help you.

Hurts and Offenses

Heavenly Father,

I need Your help to get over some hurts and offenses I have incurred. I know I shouldn't hold grudges—and I don't mean to—but sometimes the pain makes it difficult to let go. I realize, however, that holding on only hurts me more.

I choose to forgive today. I let the offenses go and pray that You will bless those who have hurt me. I receive Your healing to mend my wounds and ask You to fill me with Your love so that it overflows—even toward those who have hurt me.

In Jesus' name,
Amen.

Be even-tempered, content with second place,
quick to forgive an offense. Forgive as quickly and
completely as the Master forgave you.

COLOSSIANS 3:13 MSG

Watch out that no bitterness takes root among you,
for as it springs up it causes deep trouble,
hurting many in their spiritual lives.

HEBREWS 12:15 TLB

Never get revenge. Never hold a grudge against any of
your people. Instead, love your neighbor as you love
yourself. I am the LORD.

LEVITICUS 19:18 GWT

Love . . . is not irritable or touchy. It does not hold grudges
and will hardly even notice when others do it wrong.

1 CORINTHIANS 13:5 TLB

[Jesus said,] "Love your enemies. Let them bring out the
best in you, not the worst. When someone gives you a hard
time, respond with the energies of prayer."

MATTHEW 5:44 MSG

Forgiveness doesn't just release the offender,
it also releases you.

FIVE-YEAR-OLD LUKE WAS staying at his grandparents' house for the weekend. At dinner, out of the blue, he said, "You know, one time I broke my mom's lamp."

His grandmother asked if she was angry when it happened. "She was disappointed," Luke replied, which his grandparents assured him was understandable. But then Luke turned to his grandmother and said, "But I don't understand something. Mom says it's all been forgotten—but I can still remember it. Why can't she?"

As a mom, there's no doubt that your children have disappointed you at times—perhaps they have even deeply wounded you. Broken lamps and broken hearts. These hurts or offenses may be caused intentionally or unintentionally, but either way, the pain can be difficult to bear. It is easy to let these offenses pile up, unless you make the conscious, purposeful choice to walk in forgiveness.

It may be hard to forgive those who have caused hurt, even if they are your own children. But Jesus has given us the power to do just that through His Spirit, whose fruit includes love. (See Galatians 5:22.) One way He can grow this fruit in our lives is through prayer. When we pray for those people who hurt us, love and restoration are the eventual results. (See Matthew 5:44.)

No matter what your children—or other people—do to harm you, you can walk in unconditional love and forgiveness. Begin to pray for the one who has hurt you, and watch your attitude and your relationship be transformed by God's grace.

For what have you needed forgiveness recently?

Integrity

Father God,

My heart longs to be real, to be the person You made me to be. But in this world, that is hard. There is so much pressure to conform to a certain standard or image that is acceptable to others.

I am sorry for giving in to that pressure, Father, because it is an insult to You and Your creativity. Give me the strength to be real—a person of integrity—and help me create an environment in our home where my children feel safe to be themselves. Your unconditional love makes that possible.

In Jesus' name,
Amen.

The righteous walk in integrity—
happy are the children who follow them!

PROVERBS 20:7 NRSV

You have preserved me because I was honest; you have
admitted me forever to your presence.

PSALM 41:12 TLB

I stay true to myself.
Be kind and rescue me.

PSALM 26:11 CEV

Whoever walks in integrity walks securely.

PROVERBS 10:9 NRSV

The integrity of the upright guides them.

PROVERBS 11:3 NRSV

[Jesus said,] "Anyone who intends to come with me
has to let me lead. You're not in the driver's seat—
I am. . . . What good would it do to get everything you
want and lose you, the real you?"

LUKE 9:23, 25 MSG

*Be real—the genuine article.
Fakes are a dime a dozen. The real you is priceless.*

OF COURSE, YOU WANT YOUR CHILDREN TO BE HONEST. You don't want them to cheat, you don't want them to lie, and you don't want them to steal. And rightfully so. These are the things that come to mind when you think of integrity. But actually the biblical meaning of the word has more to do with who you are than what you do. It deals more with the issue of being genuine. That can be more challenging.

A good example would be when you go along with the crowd because you don't want to make waves even though deep inside, you don't agree. True integrity is when the "real" you is portrayed outwardly. Everyone wants to be accepted, but too often we get acceptance at the sacrifice of our true selves. We end up winning the battle but losing the war. We temporarily get our "belonging" fix, but inside we feel cheated because we are not being ourselves. We cheat others also because we are not presenting who we really are. We are in essence—get ready—lying! And most important we cheat someone else—God! He created each person uniquely with a certain purpose in mind. If we try to be someone else, we are saying to Him that what He designed has no value.

Even though being "real" is a hard task, your children will reap the benefits if you make the decision to do so. As you come to terms with your true self, you will encourage them to be the real people God meant for them to be. As they see your courage, they, too, will be inspired to risk being who they are!

Are you being your real self in every one of your relationships? If not, why?

Jealousy

Heavenly Father,

I do not like it when I become jealous or compare myself to others. It hinders me from enjoying my own blessings, and it prevents me from loving others as I should.

Forgive me, Father. You have been so good to me, and I don't ever want to take Your blessings for granted. And I realize that it is Your nature to give, so I know there are many more good things You are planning to shower on me.

I rejoice with others in their blessings and thank You for being such a good God.

In Jesus' name,
Amen.

When you are jealous and quarrel among yourselves,
aren't you influenced by your corrupt nature and
living by human standards?

1 Corinthians 3:3 gwt

Be happy with those who are happy.

Romans 12:15 gnt

Love never is envious nor boils over with jealousy.

1 Corinthians 13:4 amp

If you are bitterly jealous and filled with self-centered
ambition, don't brag. Don't say that you are wise when it
isn't true. That kind of wisdom doesn't come from above.
It belongs to this world. It is self-centered and demonic.
Wherever there is jealousy and rivalry,
there is disorder and every kind of evil.

James 3:14–16 gwt

Let us live in a right way, like people who belong to the
day. . . . There should be . . . no fighting or jealousy. But
clothe yourselves with the Lord Jesus Christ and forget
about satisfying your sinful self.

Romans 13:13–14 ncv

*The best antidote for jealousy is to count your own blessings
while rejoicing with others for the ones they receive.*

IT'S EASY TO FALL INTO THE TRAP OF COMPARING OURSELVES TO OTHERS. Maybe the family down the street buys a new car every few years, while you struggle to put food on the table. When we start down the road of making comparisons, we can find all kinds of things to be jealous of—types of jobs, houses, possessions, kids' grades, talents—the list could go on for pages. Yet when we travel this road, we begin to overlook the many blessings God has poured into our own lives.

Psalm 37 has much to say about jealousy and comparing ourselves to others. It gives this advice: "Delight yourself in the Lord and he will give you the desires of your heart. Commit your way to the Lord; trust in him. . . . Be still before the Lord and wait patiently for him" (vv. 4–5, 7 niv). It goes on to make these important promises: "If the Lord delights in a man's way, he makes his steps firm; though he stumble, he will not fall, for the Lord upholds him with his hand. I was young and now I am old, yet I have never seen the righteous forsaken or their children begging bread. They are always generous and lend freely; their children will be blessed" (vv. 23–26 niv).

Next time you're tempted to compare yourself to others, take a moment to recognize the many ways God has blessed you. When you're tempted to worry, take comfort in God's promises and know that He will take care of your every need.

What are some blessings you can be thankful for in your life?

Letting Go

Heavenly Father,

This may be the hardest thing I've ever had to do. How does a mother hen stop hovering? I know letting go is a normal—and healthy—part of life, but everything in me wants to hold on.

Of course I'll never stop being a mother, but I need Your help to adjust to each stage of letting go as it comes. Give me wisdom to know what to release to You and when to do it, and help my children and me to make each transition smoothly and with grace.

In Jesus' name,
Amen.

[Hannah said,] "For this child I prayed; and the Lord has
granted me the petition that I made to him.
Therefore I have lent him to the Lord;
as long as he lives, he is given to the Lord."

1 Samuel 1:27–28 nrsv

Let go [of your concerns!]
Then you will know that I am God.

Psalm 46:10 gwt

There's an opportune time to do things,
a right time for everything on the earth; . . .
A right time to hold on and another to let go.

Ecclesiastes 3:1, 6 msg

For this reason a man will leave his father and mother and
be united to his wife, and they will become one flesh.

Genesis 2:24 niv

[Jesus said,] "Anyone who comes to me but refuses to let
go of father, mother, spouse, children, brothers, sisters—
yes, even one's own self!—can't be my disciple."

Luke 14:26 msg

*Childbirth is the beginning of a mother's lifelong
process of letting go of her children until she finally
sends them forth as adults.*

LETTING GO. SUCH A HARD THING TO DO. But what a necessary thing it is. We play peekaboo a thousand times. We kiss boo-boos. We drop our children off at practice. We watch them in their school programs. We take pictures of them as they leave for their proms. And then the day comes when we attend their graduation. And next, marriage.

We've been with them since day one, and now we have the unsettling realization that we are relegated to just watching from now on. No longer will they be under our care—they must forge their own destinies apart from our oversight. We feel sadness.

It's a situation every parent faces sooner or later. And it's one that people deal with differently. Some attempt to hang on, maybe even try to induce guilt upon their children for wanting to sprout their wings. Some exert control by withholding acceptance or material possessions in order to keep their children under their influence. And some lovingly cut the apron strings with a tear in their eyes and wish them well.

Which kind of parent will you be when the time comes? It's best to think about it now before that fateful day arrives. As you begin to pray for God to prepare you for that day, consider this: Your children are merely on loan to you from God. They are His creation, designed for a certain task that He has assigned them. God has merely given you the privilege of preparing them for this task. A release at the end of the training has always been the goal.

This letting go won't be easy, but your children will love you for it.

What steps can you take today to begin to let go of your children? What adjustments do you need to make in order to do that?

_____

_____

_____

_____

_____

_____

_____

_____

_____

_____

_____

Praise

Heavenly Father,

You are such a good God, worthy of any and all praise I can give You. Not only do I exalt You in song and with my words, but I praise You in my attitudes and actions as well. Let everything about my life glorify You.

Cause my children to notice the example I set and to begin lifting up their voices in adoration. Your Word says that You inhabit the praises of Your people. I pray that our home will be filled with Your presence as we continually exalt Your holy name.

In Jesus' name,
Amen.

Let the word of Christ richly dwell within you, with all
wisdom teaching and admonishing one another with
psalms and hymns and spiritual songs, singing with thankfulness in your hearts to God.

Colossians 3:16 nasb

I will bless the Lord at all times:
His praise shall continually be in my mouth.

Psalm 34:1 kjv

I will give repeated thanks to the Lord,
praising him to everyone.

Psalm 109:30 tlb

Praise him for his mighty acts.
Praise him for his immense greatness. . . .
Let everything that breathes praise the Lord!

Psalm 150:2, 6 gwt

Be filled with the Spirit, speaking to one another in psalms
and hymns and spiritual songs, singing and making melody with your heart to the Lord; always giving thanks for all
things in the name of our Lord Jesus Christ to God.

Ephesians 5:18–20 nasb

*Praising the Lord for all His blessings will lighten your load
and set a great example for your children.*

TEACHING YOUR CHILDREN HOW TO PRAISE GOD is one of the greatest gifts you can bestow upon them. After all, this is one of the primary proposes for which they were created, and they'll find their greatest fulfillment in worshipping their Creator.

When an unexpected blessing comes into your life, give God glory for it in front of your children. When you're going through a difficult time, praise God for His faithfulness to carry you through life's circumstances. Make praise and thanksgiving an important part of your family prayer time, and be sure your children know how grateful you are to God for the gift He's given you in them. By doing so, you'll build their confidence and will teach them through your example how to give praise and thanks to God in the midst of any situation.

Incorporate praise to God into your children's everyday routine by playing worship music around the house or in the car. Encourage them to lift their voices in song, to make joyful noises with instruments, and to dance before their Creator, allowing them to have fun with the experience and to be themselves. As you do this, take the time to enjoy the beauty of their creativity.

Psalm 8:2 NIV says, "From the lips of children and infants you have ordained praise." It's never too early to incorporate praise into the lives of your children. By teaching your children how to offer praise to God, you are helping them to fulfill one of their greatest callings in life—to bring praise, glory, and honor to their Heavenly Father.

What are some fun and creative ways you can incorporate praise into your routine today?

Pregnancy

Heavenly Father,

Having a child is one of life's most precious blessings. I pray that my body would be strong and that You would bless all of my organs and cause them to function as You designed them to. I pray that my hormones would be balanced and that the joy of the Lord would be my strength.

Thank You that You knit my child inside my womb and cause this little one to be healthy and whole and to come forth at the proper time. Even now I dedicate my precious child to You.

In Jesus' name,
Amen.

[The Lord God] will feed His flock like a shepherd;
He will gather the lambs with His arm,
and carry them in His bosom,
And gently lead those who are with young.

Isaiah 40:11 nkjv

You shall worship the Lord your God, and I will bless your
bread and your water; and I will take sickness away from
among you. No one shall miscarry or be barren in your
land; I will fulfill the number of your days.

Exodus 23:25–26 nrsv

May the God of your fathers, the Almighty, bless you
with blessings of heaven above and of the earth beneath—
blessings of the breasts and of the womb.

Genesis 49:25 tlb

The Lord spoke these words to me:
"Before I made you in your mother's womb, I chose you.
Before you were born, I set you apart for a special work."

Jeremiah 1:4–5 icb

*No privilege can compare to carrying a child and knowing
that you have had a role in the creation of a living being.*

❋

CHILDREN ARE A BLESSING OF THE LORD! If you're a mom already, you know that. And if you are going to become a mom soon, it won't be long before you experience the joy that only children can bring.

Pregnancy can be a joyful time, but it can be a challenging time as well. A dramatically changing body is just the beginning of the exciting, yet sometimes stressful changes that lie ahead.

If you are feeling a bit overwhelmed by what is taking place, remember that God is the One who has created your baby, who is molding and shaping your new son or daughter in your womb. The Bible says of our Heavenly Father: "You created my inmost being; you knit me together in my mother's womb" (Psalm 139:13 NIV). God has a plan for both you and your baby, and He will see it through to its completion.

If you want more children but have been unable to conceive, remember all the women in Scripture who had problems conceiving a child, but who were blessed with motherhood through God's healing power. Sarah, Rachel, Hannah, and Elizabeth all bore "miracle babies" because God touched their lives.

No matter what your situation may be, you can place

your future and the future of your unborn children in God's hands. As a future mother, you will be able to say, as Hannah did, "For this child I prayed, and the Lord has granted me my petition which I asked of Him" (1 Samuel 1:27 NKJV). God is faithful to His Word, and He will keep both you and your children in His care.

How many children do you have? How many would you like to have?

_____

_____

_____

_____

_____

_____

_____

_____

_____

_____

Purpose

Father God,

Amid the busyness of everyday life and the mundane responsibilities of mothering, it is often difficult to have a clear sense of purpose. Somehow the sense of destiny gets lost in the mountains of laundry and grocery shopping.

Of course mothering is a high calling, but I'm needing help to see the big picture right now. What role are my unique gifts and talents to play in my children's lives? Help me to see not only the trees but the whole forest. Having clear purpose will help me invest myself fully and with joy.

In Jesus' name,
Amen.

In him we were also chosen, having been predestined
according to the plan of him who works out everything in
conformity with the purpose of his will.

Ephesians 1:11 niv

God is always at work in you to make you willing
and able to obey his own purpose.

Philippians 2:13 gnt

The Lord will fulfill his purpose for me;
your steadfast love, O Lord, endures forever.

Psalm 138:8 nrsv

Each one has his own gift from God,
one in this manner and another in that.

1 Corinthians 7:7 nkjv

We are His workmanship, created in Christ Jesus
for good works, which God prepared beforehand
that we should walk in them.

Ephesians 2:10 nkjv

There is no greater purpose than to raise a child.

THE FAMOUS ENGLISH SCULPTOR HENRY MOORE WAS ONCE ASKED A FASCINATING QUESTION by a literary critic: "Now that you are eighty, you must know the secret of life. What is it?"

Moore paused ever so slightly, with just enough time to smile before answering. "The secret of life," he mused, "is to have a task, something you do your entire life, something you bring everything to, every minute of your day for your whole life. And the most important thing is: It must be something you cannot possibly do."

Henry Moore was not a mother, but it seems like he understood the purpose of moms very well. The task of raising children may seem daunting, but it is also a God-given challenge, a sacred trust issued to you because of God's faith in your ability to do it—with help from Him. And contrary to feelings of inadequacy that you may sometimes have, God has equipped you for this task.

However, God also created you to be more than just a mother. He created you to be uniquely you—with special gifts and talents to be used for His kingdom and His glory. Even when your children are young, you must remember that you are more than just a bottle-washer or a diaper-changer. You are shaping the generation of tomorrow—and that matters a great deal to God and to this world.

God knows the plans He has for you—they are good plans, to give you hope, and a future beyond your imagination. (See Jeremiah 29:11.) You are here for a purpose!

What is your purpose in life?

Single Mom

Dear God,

I wouldn't trade my children for anything in the world, but sometimes being a single mom is overwhelming and lonely. If ever I needed You, it is now.

Be a husband to me, God. Be my sounding board, the One I turn to when I need advice. Lead me when I don't know which way to go, and comfort me when I need a shoulder to cry on. Be the lover of my soul, my companion and friend. And be a Father to my children, that they may know and love You as I do.

In Jesus' name,
Amen.

He [God] Himself has said, I will not in any way fail you
nor give you up nor leave you without support.
[I will] not, [I will] not, [I will] not in any degree leave
you helpless nor forsake nor let [you] down (relax My hold
on you)! [Assuredly not!] So we take comfort and
are encouraged and confidently and boldly say,
The Lord is my Helper; I will not be seized with alarm
[I will not fear or dread or be terrified].

HEBREWS 13:5–6 AMP

Fear not [there is nothing to fear], for I am with you;
do not look around you in terror and be dismayed,
for I am your God. I will strengthen and harden you to
difficulties, yes, I will help you; yes, I will hold you up
and retain you with My [victorious] right hand.

ISAIAH 41:10 AMP

"Don't be embarrassed, because you will not be disgraced.
You will forget the shame you felt earlier;
you will not remember the shame you felt when you lost
your husband. The God who made you is like your husband. His name is the LORD All-Powerful."

ISAIAH 54:4–5 NCV

*God will be a husband to you—if you let Him.
He won't let you down.*

JOAN'S WORLD CAME CRASHING DOWN AROUND HER when she discovered her husband was addicted to prescription drugs. He began using family funds to support his habit. He also started seeing another woman. His whole life spiraled out of control.

Months later, Joan found herself in the middle of a nasty divorce with two small children. Her life had changed from one of security to barely making ends meet. And the utter exhaustion of raising and caring for two little ones, while at the same time trying to make a living, was taking its toll on her. She was angry, tired, and feeling pretty hopeless.

But as months turned into a year and then two, she sought God with all her heart. Although, at first, she longed to be married again, that door remained closed. She came to the place where she trusted God and made Him the "man" in her life. God miraculously provided for all of her and her kids' needs. The struggles were real, but God met them at every turn.

So, how did Joan's story turn out? Today, Joan is happily married to a wonderful, stable Christian man who has wholeheartedly accepted the role of father to her children. The whole family prays together and plays together.

If you're a single mom, let Joan's story encourage you.

God gave her strength and courage when she was at her lowest. Your desires may be different from hers. But God wants to help you care for your children and He wants to be there for you as well. You are NOT alone!

What are your greatest needs as a single mom? Cry out to the Lord to meet those needs.

Speaking Kind Words

Heavenly Father,

My words have such a powerful effect on my children, and I am not always happy with what I hear coming out of my mouth.

Father, help me put a guard over my mouth and cause me to be more aware of what I say before I say it. When I begin to say something unkind, bring a better choice of words to mind. I am committed to speaking positive words of life to my children, words that will build them up and cause them to be champions for Christ. Thank You for helping me.

In Jesus' name,
Amen.

Death and life are in the power of the tongue.

Proverbs 18:21 nkjv

When [a good woman] speaks she has something
worthwhile to say, and she always says it kindly.

Proverbs 31:26 msg

When you talk, do not say harmful things. But say what
people need—words that will help others become stronger.

Ephesians 4:29 icb

A good person's words are a fountain of life.

Proverbs 10:11 gnt

Thoughtless words can wound as deeply as any sword,
but wisely spoken words can heal.

Proverbs 12:18 gnt

Be gracious in your speech. The goal is to bring out the
best in others in a conversation, not put them down.

Colossians 4:6 msg

*Kind words can be short and easy to speak,
but their echoes are truly endless.*

Mother Teresa of Calcutta

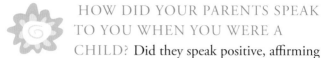 HOW DID YOUR PARENTS SPEAK TO YOU WHEN YOU WERE A CHILD? Did they speak positive, affirming words; or were their words a source of pain and rejection?

We usually follow in the footsteps of our parents when it comes to parenting style. And that's good if you grew up in a positive environment. But beware if you're following the trail of a parent who was verbally abusive.

Words are powerful containers. The Bible says they are filled with either life or death. Your words can bring hope or discouragement to your children—the choice is yours. From the time children are born, they gather all their information about themselves and their world from their parents—parents are their source for everything. If parents speak words of love and acceptance, their children will internalize that acceptance and believe in their own value. On the other hand, if parents say things like, "You'll never amount to anything," their children will internalize that message and doubt their own value. Your input as a parent is paramount since your children spend so much time with you. So, positive words and attitudes from you are crucial to their well-being and success.

Of course, you want your children to succeed in life. Begin today to speak kind words. When you fail, don't be afraid to apologize to your children. It will cause them to respect you more and will heal their hearts from your harsh words.

If you grew up under a harsh parent yourself, you may not know how to treat your children with respect. If this is the case, seek help. God loves you, and He wants to help you and your children.

Are you speaking kind words to your children? If not, go to them and tell them you are sorry. Then make a decision to speak only positive words.

Success

Heavenly Father,

I want my children and me to be healthy and whole and to enjoy success in all that we do. But I want that success to be in line with Your definition of it. Open our eyes to view it through Your eyes.

Father, help us to be responsible and diligent, but to also enjoy the journey so we can experience "abundant life" to the fullest. Remind us to savor the special moments each day even in the midst of our busyness so we can rejoice in the success that You grant us.

In Jesus' name,
Amen.

"How great is the LORD!
He is pleased with the success of his servant."

PSALM 35:27 GNT

"It's not possible for a person to succeed—I'm talking
about eternal success—without heaven's help."

JOHN 3:27 MSG

Enjoy all the days of this short life God has given you here
on earth. It is all you have. So enjoy the work you have to
do here on earth. Whatever work you do, do your best.

ECCLESIASTES 9:9–10 ICB

Good people enjoy success.

PROVERBS 13:21 ICB

"This book of the law shall not depart from your mouth,
but you shall meditate on it day and night, so that you may
be careful to do according to all that is written in it;
for then you will make your way prosperous,
and then you will have success."

JOSHUA 1:8 NASB

*He has achieved success who has lived well, laughed often,
and loved much . . . whose life was an inspiration;
whose memory a benediction.*

BESSIE ANDERSON STANLEY

ARCHITECT FRANK LLOYD WRIGHT ONCE TOLD of an incident that seemed insignificant at the time, but had a profound influence on the rest of his life. The winter he was nine, he went walking across a snow-covered field with his reserved, no-nonsense uncle. As the two of them reached the far end of the field, his uncle stopped him. He pointed out his own tracks in the snow, straight and true as an arrow's flight, and then young Frank's tracks meandering all over the field. "Notice how your tracks wander aimlessly from the fence to the cattle to the woods and back again," his uncle said. "And see how my tracks aim directly to my goal. There is an important lesson in that."

Years later the world-famous architect liked to tell how this experience contributed to his philosophy in life. "I determined right then," he'd say with a twinkle in his eye, "not to miss most things in life, as my uncle had."

As a mom, what is your idea of success? Sometimes success might be just getting through the day with everyone fed, clothed, and sane—including yourself! But there is more to being a parent than just the basics. In the midst of all the busyness of getting things done, don't forget to explore life with your children. Don't just rush through the field in order to achieve your goal of reaching the other side.

Success in parenting does involve raising happy, healthy kids into adults who love God and who are productive in society. Like Jesus, they should grow in "wisdom and stature, and in favor with God and men" (Luke 2:52 NIV). But you should also make it your goal to have some fun along the way!

How can you begin to explore life more fully with your children?

_____

_____

_____

_____

_____

_____

_____

_____

_____

_____

_____

_____

Teaching Forgiveness

Father in Heaven,

Forgiveness is one of the most important lessons I can teach my children. Help me first to set a good example. Then lead me as I teach them from Your Word about how readily You forgive us and how important it is that they forgive others.

When my children suffer wrongs, give me wisdom on how to use each instance as an opportunity to grow. Give them tender hearts that are quick to pardon instead of bearing grudges or seeking revenge. Then bless them with sweet release as they let their offenders go.

In Jesus' name,
Amen.

"Whenever you pray, forgive anything you have against anyone. Then your Father in heaven will forgive your failures."

MARK 11:25 GWT

[Jesus said,] "Forgive, and you will be forgiven."

LUKE 6:37 GWT

Put up with each other, and forgive anyone who does you wrong, just as Christ has forgiven you. Love is more important than anything else. It is what ties everything completely together.

COLOSSIANS 3:13–14 CEV

[Jesus said,] "Be alert. If you see your friend going wrong, correct him. If he responds, forgive him. Even if it's personal against you and repeated seven times through the day, and seven times he says, 'I'm sorry, I won't do it again,' forgive him."

LUKE 17:3–4 MSG

God pardons like a mother,
who kisses the offense into everlasting forgiveness.

HENRY WARD BEECHER

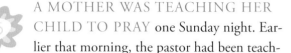 A MOTHER WAS TEACHING HER CHILD TO PRAY one Sunday night. Earlier that morning, the pastor had been teaching on the Lord's Prayer, and so the four-year-old bowed his head and tried to repeat what he had learned: "And forgive us our trash baskets as we forgive those who put trash in our baskets."

That may seem amusing to us at first, but it's really true, isn't it? We all have "trash" in our lives—junk for which we need to be forgiven, often many times for the same thing. But then there are the times when others put their "trash" in our "baskets"—and we ourselves have to learn how to forgive.

Forgiveness isn't easy for adults to practice—let alone consistently demonstrating it to a child. It's often very difficult for us to be good models of forgiveness for our children. But that is the best way to teach forgiveness—by practicing it yourself. That's what Jesus did. He told us to forgive our neighbors, and then He practiced the ultimate act of forgiveness by forgiving His enemies even as He was dying on the cross.

Although forgiveness may be difficult, it is one of the most important things you can teach your child. Someone once said: "The sin of unforgiveness is a cancer that destroys relationships, eats away at one's own psyche, and—worst of all—shuts us off from God's grace." Make sure your children understand the importance of forgiving other people, and help them learn by practicing it in your own life. You'll both be glad that you did!

How can you demonstrate forgiveness to your child today?

_____

_____

_____

_____

_____

_____

_____

_____

_____

_____

_____

_____

_____

_____

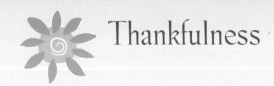

Thankfulness

Heavenly Father,

Forgive me for the times that I have been less than thankful. You have blessed me in so many ways, not the least of which is through the gift of my children. I am forever grateful for the privilege of helping them to fulfill their destiny.

Thank You, too, for the multitude of other ways You have blessed me. To live in a free country, to have the necessities of life, to love and be loved—by You and others—are precious gifts that I do not take for granted.

Thank You, precious Father.

In Jesus' name,

Amen.

Give thanks to the LORD, call on his name;
make known among the nations what he has done.

PSALM 105:1 NIV

Do you see what we've got? An unshakable kingdom! And
do you see how thankful we must be? Not only thankful,
but brimming with worship, deeply reverent before God.

HEBREWS 12:28 MSG

God, I will thank you forever for what you have done.
With those who worship you, I will trust you
because you are good.

PSALM 52:9 ICB

I will give thanks to you
because I have been so amazingly and miraculously made.

PSALM 139:14 GWT

Beloved . . . if there is any excellence and if there is
anything worthy of praise, think about these things.

PHILIPPIANS 4:8 NRSV

Nothing is more honorable than a grateful heart.

SENECA

DID YOU KNOW THAT THE WORDS *THINK* AND *THANK* COME FROM the same root word, reminding us that thanksgiving comes from thinking about our blessings?

Senator Richard Neuberger described how the experience of contracting cancer changed him: "A change came over me which I believe is irreversible. Questions of prestige, of political success, of financial status, became all at once unimportant. In their stead has come a new appreciation of things I once took for granted—eating lunch with a friend, scratching Muffet's ears and listening for his purr, the company of my wife, reading a book or magazine in the quiet cone of my bed lamp at night, raiding the refrigerator for a glass of orange juice or a slice of coffee cake. For the first time I think I am actually savoring life."

God loves it when His children cultivate an attitude of thanksgiving to Him for all that He has given them. Are you thankful for your husband and children? Are you grateful for the roof over your head, clothes to wear, and food to eat? Most of all, aren't you filled with gratitude for the priceless gift Jesus paid for your salvation on the cross?

It can be easy to lose sight of all the blessings we have

been given—but it's just as easy to get back on track with our thankfulness. Just think of all the ways you have been blessed, and then thank the One who showers you with those blessings each day.

How are you "savoring life"?

Read through the Bible in a Year Plan

January

1 Genesis 1:1–2:25; Matthew 1:1–2:12; Psalm 1:1–6; Proverbs 1:1–6
2 Genesis 3:1–4:26; Matthew 2:13–3:6; Psalm 2:1–12; Proverbs 1:7–9
3 Genesis 5:1–7:24; Matthew 3:7–4:11; Psalm 3:1–8; Proverbs 1:10–19
4 Genesis 8:1–10:32; Matthew 4:12–25; Psalm 4:1–8; Proverbs 1:20–23
5 Genesis 11:1–13:4; Matthew 5:1–26; Psalm 5:1–12; Proverbs 1:24–28
6 Genesis 13:5–15:21; Matthew 5:27–48; Psalm 6:1–10; Proverbs 1:29–33
7 Genesis 16:1–18:15; Matthew 6:1–24; Psalm 7:1–17; Proverbs 2:1–5
8 Genesis 18:16–19:38; Matthew 6:25–7:14; Psalm 8:1–9; Proverbs 2:6–15
9 Genesis 20:1–22:24; Matthew 7:15–29; Psalm 9:1–12; Proverbs 2:16–22
10 Genesis 23:1–24:51; Matthew 8:1–17; Psalm 9:13–20; Proverbs 3:1–6
11 Genesis 24:52–26:16; Matthew 8:18–34; Psalm 10:1–15; Proverbs 3:7–8
12 Genesis 26:17–27:46; Matthew 9:1–17; Psalm 10:16–18; Proverbs 3:9–10
13 Genesis 28:1–29:35; Matthew 9:18–38; Psalm 11:1–7; Proverbs 3:11–12
14 Genesis 30:1–31:16; Matthew 10:1–23; Psalm 12:1–8; Proverbs 3:13–15
15 Genesis 31:17–32:12; Matthew 10:24–11:6; Psalm 13:1–6; Proverbs 3:16–18
16 Genesis 32:13–34:31; Matthew 11:7–30; Psalm 14:1–7; Proverbs 3:19–20
17 Genesis 35:1–36:43; Matthew 12:1–21; Psalm 15:1–5; Proverbs 3:21–26
18 Genesis 37:1–38:30; Matthew 12:22–45; Psalm 16:1–11; Proverbs 3:27–32
19 Genesis 39:1–41:16; Matthew 12:46–13:23; Psalm 17:1–15; Proverbs 3:33–35
20 Genesis 41:17–42:17; Matthew 13:24–46; Psalm 18:1–15; Proverbs 4:1–6
21 Genesis 42:18–43:34; Matthew 13:47–14:12; Psalm 18:16–36; Proverbs 4:7–10
22 Genesis 44:1–45:28; Matthew 14:13–36; Psalm 18:37–50; Proverbs 4:11–13
23 Genesis 46:1–47:31; Matthew 15:1–28; Psalm 19:1–14; Proverbs 4:14 –19
24 Genesis 48:1–49:33; Matthew 15:29–16:12; Psalm 20:1–9; Proverbs 4:20–27
25 Genesis 50:1–Exodus 2:10; Matthew 16:13–17:9; Psalm 21:1–13; Proverbs 5:1–6
26 Exodus 2:11–3:22; Matthew 17:10–27; Psalm 22:1–18; Proverbs 5:7–14
27 Exodus 4:1–5:21; Matthew 18:1–20; Psalm 22:19–31; Proverbs 5:15–21
28 Exodus 5:22–7:25; Matthew 18:21–19:12; Psalm 23:1–6; Proverbs 5:22–23
29 Exodus 8:1–9:35; Matthew 19:13–30; Psalm 24:1–10; Proverbs 6:1–5
30 Exodus 10:1–12:13; Matthew 20:1–28; Psalm 25:1–15; Proverbs 6:6–11
31 Exodus 12:14–13:16; Matthew 20:29–21:22; Psalm 25:16–22; Proverbs 6:12–15

February

 1 Exodus 13:17–15:18; Matthew 21:23–46; Psalm 26:1–12; Proverbs 6:16–19
 2 Exodus 15:19–17:7; Matthew 22:1–33; Psalm 27:1–6; Proverbs 6:20–26
 3 Exodus 17:8–19:15; Matthew 22:34–23:12; Psalm 27:7–14; Proverbs 6:27–35
 4 Exodus 19:16–21:21; Matthew 23:13–39; Psalm 28:1–9; Proverbs 7:1–5
 5 Exodus 21:22–23:13; Matthew 24:1–28; Psalm 29:1–11; Proverbs 7:6–23
 6 Exodus 23:14–25:40; Matthew 24:29–51; Psalm 30:1–12; Proverbs 7:24–27
 7 Exodus 26:1–27:21; Matthew 25:1–30; Psalm 31:1–8; Proverbs 8:1–11
 8 Exodus 28:1–43; Matthew 25:31–26:13; Psalm 31:9–18; Proverbs 8:12–13
 9 Exodus 29:1–30:10; Matthew 26:14–46; Psalm 31:19–24; Proverbs 8:14–26
10 Exodus 30:11–31:18; Matthew 26:47–68; Psalm 32:1–11; Proverbs 8:27–32
11 Exodus 32:1–33:23; Matthew 26:69–27:14; Psalm 33:1–11; Proverbs 8:33–36
12 Exodus 34:1–35:9; Matthew 27:15–31; Psalm 33:12–22; Proverbs 9:1–6
13 Exodus 35:10–36:38; Matthew 27:32–66; Psalm 34:1–10; Proverbs 9:7–8
14 Exodus 37:1–38:31; Matthew 28:1–20; Psalm 34:11–22; Proverbs 9:9–10
15 Exodus 39:1–40:38; Mark 1:1–28; Psalm 35:1–16; Proverbs 9:11–12
16 Leviticus 1:1–3:17; Mark 1:29–2:12; Psalm 35:17–28; Proverbs 9:13–18
17 Leviticus 4:1–5:19; Mark 2:13–3:6; Psalm 36:1–12; Proverbs 10:1–2
18 Leviticus 6:1–7:27; Mark 3:7–30; Psalm 37:1–11; Proverbs 10:3–4
19 Leviticus 7:28–9:6; Mark 3:31–4:25; Psalm 37:12–29; Proverbs 10:5
20 Leviticus 9:7–10:20; Mark 4:26–5:20; Psalm 37:30–40; Proverbs 10:6–7
21 Leviticus 11:1–12:8; Mark 5:21–43; Psalm 38:1–22; Proverbs 10:8–9
22 Leviticus 13:1–59; Mark 6:1–29; Psalm 39:1–13; Proverbs 10:10
23 Leviticus 14:1–57; Mark 6:30–56; Psalm 40:1–10; Proverbs 10:11–12
24 Leviticus 15:1–16:28; Mark 7:1–23; Psalm 40:11–17; Proverbs 10:13–14
25 Leviticus 16:29–18:30; Mark 7:24–8:10; Psalm 41:1–13; Proverbs 10:15–16
26 Leviticus 19:1–20:21; Mark 8:11–38; Psalm 42:1–11; Proverbs 10:17
27 Leviticus 20:22–22:16; Mark 9:1–29; Psalm 43:1–5; Proverbs 10:18
28 Leviticus 22:17–23:44; Mark 9:30–10:12; Psalm 44:1–8; Proverbs 10:19

March

1 Leviticus 24:1–25:46; Mark 10:13–31; Psalm 44:9–26; Proverbs 10:20–21

2 Leviticus 25:47–27:13; Mark 10:32–52; Psalm 45:1–17; Proverbs 10:22

3 Leviticus 27:14–Numbers 1:54; Mark 11:1–26; Psalm 46:1–11; Proverbs 10:23

4 Numbers 2:1–3:51; Mark 11:27–12:17; Psalm 47:1–9; Proverbs 10:24–25

5 Numbers 4:1–5:31; Mark 12:18–37; Psalm 48:1–14; Proverbs 10:26

6 Numbers 6:1–7:89; Mark 12:38–13:13; Psalm 49:1–20; Proverbs 10:27–28

7 Numbers 8:1–9:23; Mark 13:14–37; Psalm 50:1–23; Proverbs 10:29–30

8 Numbers 10:1–11:23; Mark 14:1–21; Psalm 51:1–19; Proverbs 10:31–32

9 Numbers 11:24–13:33; Mark 14:22–52; Psalm 52:1–9; Proverbs 11:1–3

10 Numbers 14:1–15:16; Mark 14:53–72; Psalm 53:1–6; Proverbs 11:4

11 Numbers 15:17–16:40; Mark 15:1–47; Psalm 54:1–7; Proverbs 11:5–6

12 Numbers 16:41–18:32; Mark 16:1–20; Psalm 55:1–23; Proverbs 11:7

13 Numbers 19:1–20:29; Luke 1:1–25; Psalm 56:1–13; Proverbs 11:8

14 Numbers 21:1–22:20; Luke 1:26–56; Psalm 57:1–11; Proverbs 11:9–11

15 Numbers 22:21–23:30; Luke 1:57–80; Psalm 58:1–11; Proverbs 11:12–13

16 Numbers 24:1–25:18; Luke 2:1–35; Psalm 59:1–17; Proverbs 11:14

17 Numbers 26:1–51; Luke 2:36–52; Psalm 60:1–12; Proverbs 11:15

18 Numbers 26:52–28:15; Luke 3:1–22; Psalm 61:1–8; Proverbs 11:16–17

19 Numbers 28:16–29:40; Luke 3:23–38; Psalm 62:1–12; Proverbs 11:18–19

20 Numbers 30:1–31:54; Luke 4:1–30; Psalm 63:1–11; Proverbs 11:20–21

21 Numbers 32:1–33:39; Luke 4:31–5:11; Psalm 64:1–10; Proverbs 11:22

22 Numbers 33:40–35:34; Luke 5:12–28; Psalm 65:1–13; Proverbs 11:23

23 Numbers 36:1–Deuteronomy 1:46; Luke 5:29–6:11; Psalm 66:1–20; Proverbs 11:24–26

24 Deuteronomy 2:1–3:29; Luke 6:12–38; Psalm 67:1–7; Proverbs 11:27

25 Deuteronomy 4:1–49; Luke 6:39–7:10; Psalm 68:1–18; Proverbs 11:28

26 Deuteronomy 5:1–6:25; Luke 7:11–35; Psalm 68:19–35; Proverbs 11:29–31

27 Deuteronomy 7:1–8:20; Luke 7:36–8:3; Psalm 69:1–18; Proverbs 12:1

28 Deuteronomy 9:1–10:22; Luke 8:4–21; Psalm 69:19–36; Proverbs 12:2–3

29 Deuteronomy 11:1–12:32; Luke 8:22–39; Psalm 70:1–5; Proverbs 12:4

30 Deuteronomy 13:1–15:23; Luke 8:40–9:6; Psalm 71:1–24; Proverbs 12:5–7

31 Deuteronomy 16:1–17:20; Luke 9:7–27; Psalm 72:1–20; Proverbs 12:8–9

April

1 Deuteronomy 18:1–20:20; Luke 9:28–50; Psalm 73:1–28; Proverbs 12:10

2 Deuteronomy 21:1–22:30; Luke 9:51–10:12; Psalm 74:1–23; Proverbs 12:11

3 Deuteronomy 23:1–25:19; Luke 10:13–37; Psalm 75:1–10; Proverbs 12:12–14

4 Deuteronomy 26:1–27:26; Luke 10:38–11:13; Psalm 76:1–12; Proverbs 12:15–17

5 Deuteronomy 28:1–68; Luke 11:14–36; Psalm 77:1–20; Proverbs 12:18

6 Deuteronomy 29:1–30:20; Luke 11:37–12:7; Psalm 78:1–31; Proverbs 12:19–20

7 Deuteronomy 31:1–32:27; Luke 12:8–34; Psalm 78:32–55; Proverbs 12:21–23

8 Deuteronomy 32:28–52; Luke 12:35–59; Psalm 78:56–64; Proverbs 12:24

9 Deuteronomy 33:1–29; Luke 13:1–21; Psalm 78:65–72; Proverbs 12:25

10 Deuteronomy 34:1–Joshua 2:24; Luke 13:22–14:6; Psalm 79:1–13; Proverbs 12:26

11 Joshua 3:1–4:24; Luke 14:7–35; Psalm 80:1–19; Proverbs 12:27–28

12 Joshua 5:1–7:15; Luke 15:1–32; Psalm 81:1–16; Proverbs 13:1

13 Joshua 7:16–9:2; Luke 16:1–18; Psalm 82:1–8; Proverbs 13:2–3

14 Joshua 9:3–10:43; Luke 16:19–17:10; Psalm 83:1–18; Proverbs 13:4

15 Joshua 11:1–12:24; Luke 17:11–37; Psalm 84:1–12; Proverbs 13:5–6

16 Joshua 13:1–14:15; Luke 18:1–17; Psalm 85:1–13; Proverbs 13:7–8

17 Joshua 15:1–63; Luke 18:18–43; Psalm 86:1–17; Proverbs 13:9–10

18 Joshua 16:1–18:28; Luke 19:1–27; Psalm 87:1–7; Proverbs 13:11

19 Joshua 19:1–20:9; Luke 19:28–48; Psalm 88:1–18; Proverbs 13:12–14

20 Joshua 21:1–22:20; Luke 20:1–26; Psalm 89:1–13; Proverbs 13:15–16

21 Joshua 22:21–23:16; Luke 20:27–47; Psalm 89:14–37; Proverbs 13:17–19

22 Joshua 24:1–33; Luke 21:1–28; Psalm 89:38–52; Proverbs 13:20–23

23 Judges 1:1–2:9; Luke 21:29–22:13; Psalm 90:1–91:16; Proverbs 13:24–25

24 Judges 2:10–3:31; Luke 22:14–34; Psalm 92:1–93:5; Proverbs 14:1–2

25 Judges 4:1–5:31; Luke 22:35–53; Psalm 94:1–23; Proverbs 14:3–4

26 Judges 6:1–40; Luke 22:54–23:12; Psalm 95:1–96:13; Proverbs 14:5–6

27 Judges 7:1–8:17; Luke 23:13–43; Psalm 97:1–98:9; Proverbs 14:7–8

28 Judges 8:18–9:21; Luke 23:44–24:12; Psalm 99:1–9; Proverbs 14:9–10

29 Judges 9:22–10:18; Luke 24:13–53; Psalm 100:1–5; Proverbs 14:11–12

30 Judges 11:1–12:15; John 1:1–28; Psalm 101:1–8; Proverbs 14:13–14

May

1 Judges 13:1–14:20; John 1:29–51; Psalm 102:1–28; Proverbs 14:15–16
2 Judges 15: 1–16:31; John 2:1–25; Psalm 103:1–22; Proverbs 14:17–19
3 Judges 17:1–18:31; John 3:1–21; Psalm 104:1–23; Proverbs 14:20–21
4 Judges 19:1–20:48; John 3:22–4:3; Psalm 104:24–35; Proverbs 14:22–24
5 Judges 21:1–Ruth 1:22; John 4:4–42; Psalm 105:1–15; Proverbs 14:25
6 Ruth 2:1–4:22; John 4:43–54; Psalm 105:16–36; Proverbs 14:26–27
7 1 Samuel 1:1–2:21; John 5:1–23; Psalm 105:37–45; Proverbs 14:28–29
8 1 Samuel 2:22–4:22; John 5:24–47; Psalm 106:1–12; Proverbs 14:30–31
9 1 Samuel 5:1–7:17; John 6:1–21; Psalm 106:13–31; Proverbs 14:32–33
10 1 Samuel 8:1–9:27; John 6:22–42; Psalm 106:32–48; Proverbs 14:34–35
11 1 Samuel 10:1–11:15; John 6:43–71; Psalm 107:1–43; Proverbs 15:1–3
12 1 Samuel 12:1–13:23; John 7:1–30; Psalm 108:1–13; Proverbs 15:4
13 1 Samuel 14:1–52; John 7:31–53; Psalm 109:1–31; Proverbs 15:5–7
14 1 Samuel 15:1–16:23; John 8:1–20; Psalm 110:1–7; Proverbs15:8–10
15 1 Samuel 17:1–18:4; John 8:21–30; Psalm 111:1–10; Proverbs 15:11
16 1 Samuel 18:5–19:24; John 8:31–59; Psalm 112:1–10; Proverbs 15:12–14
17 1 Samuel 20:1–21:15; John 9:1–41; Psalm 113:1–114:8; Proverbs 15:15–17
18 1 Samuel 22:1–23:29; John 10:1–21; Psalm 115:1–18; Proverbs 15:18–19
19 1 Samuel 24:1–25:44; John 10:22–42; Psalm 116:1–19; Proverbs 15:20–21
20 1 Samuel 26:1–28:25; John 11:1–54; Psalm 117:1–2; Proverbs 15:22–23
21 1 Samuel 29:1–31:13; John 11: 55–12:19; Psalm 118:1–18; Proverbs 15:24–26
22 2 Samuel 1:1–2:11; John 12:20–50; Psalm 118:19–29: Proverbs 15:27–28
23 2 Samuel 2:12–3:39; John 13:1–30; Psalm 119:1–16; Proverbs 15:29–30
24 2 Samuel 4:1–6:23; John 13:31–14:14; Psalm 119:17–32; Proverbs 15:31–32
25 2 Samuel 7:1–8:18; John 14:15–31; Psalm 119:33–48; Proverbs 15:33
26 2 Samuel 9:1–11:27; John 15:1–27; Psalm 119:49–64; Proverbs 16:1–3
27 2 Samuel 12:1–31; John 16: 1–33; Psalm 119:65–80; Proverbs 16:4–5
28 2 Samuel 13:1–39; John 17:1–26; Psalm 119:81–96; Proverbs 16:6–7
29 2 Samuel 14:1–15:22; John 18:1–24; Psalm 119:97–112; Proverbs 16:8–9
30 2 Samuel 15:23–16:23; John 18:25–19:22; Psalm 119:113–128; Proverbs 16:10–11
31 2 Samuel 17:1–29; John 19:23–42; Psalm 119:129–152; Proverbs 16:12–13

June

1 2 Samuel 18:1–19:10; John 20:1–31; Psalm 119:153–176; Proverbs 16:14–15
2 2 Samuel 19:11–20:13; John 21:1–25; Psalm 120:1–7; Proverbs 16:16–17
3 2 Samuel 20:14–21:22; Acts 1:1–26; Psalm 121:1–8; Proverbs 16:18
4 2 Samuel 22:1–23:23; Acts 2:1–47; Psalm 122:1–9; Proverbs 16:19–20
5 2 Samuel 23:3–24:25; Acts 3:1–26; Psalm 123:1–4; Proverbs 16:21–23
6 1 Kings 1:1–53; Acts 4:1–37; Psalm 124:1–8; Proverbs 16:24
7 1 Kings 2:1–3:2; Acts 5:1–42; Psalm 125:1–5; Proverbs 16:25
8 1 Kings 3:3–4:34; Acts 6:1–15; Psalm 126:1–6; Proverbs 16:26–27
9 1 Kings 5:1–6:38; Acts 7:1–29; Psalm 127:1–5; Proverbs 16:28–30
10 1 Kings 7:1–51; Acts 7:30–50; Psalm 128:1–6; Proverbs 16:31–33
11 1 Kings 8:1–66; Acts 7:51–8:13; Psalm 129:1–8; Proverbs 17:1
12 1 Kings 9:1–10:29; Acts 8:14–40; Psalm 130:1–8; Proverbs 17:2–3
13 1 Kings 11:1–12:19; Acts 9:1–25; Psalm 131:1–3; Proverbs 17:4–5
14 1 Kings 12:20–13:34; Acts 9:26–43; Psalm 132:1–18; Proverbs 17:6
15 1 Kings 14:1–15:24; Acts 10:1:23; Psalm 133:1–3; Proverbs 17:7–8
16 1 Kings 15:25–17:24; Acts 10:24–48; Psalm 134:1–3; Proverbs 17:9–11
17 1 Kings 18:1–46; Acts 11:1–30; Psalm 135:1–21; Proverbs 17:12–13
18 1 Kings 19:1–21; Acts 12:1–23; Psalm 136:1–26; Proverbs 17:14–15
19 1 Kings 20:1–21:29; Acts 12:24–13:15; Psalm 137:1–9; Proverbs 17:16
20 1 Kings 22:1–53; Acts 13:16–41; Psalm 138:1–8; Proverbs 17:17–18
21 2 Kings 1:1–2:25; Acts 13:42–14:7; Psalm 139:1–24; Proverbs 17:19–21
22 2 Kings 3:1–4:17; Acts 14:8–28; Psalm 140:1–13; Proverbs 17:22
23 2 Kings 4:18–5:27; Acts 15:1–35; Psalm 141:1–10; Proverbs 17:23
24 2 Kings 6:1–7:20; Acts 15:36–16:15; Psalm 142:1–7; Proverbs 17:24–25
25 2 Kings 8:1–9:13; Acts 16:16–40; Psalm 143:1–12; Proverbs 17:26
26 2 Kings 9:14–10:31; Acts 17:1–34; Psalm 144:1–15; Proverbs 17:27–28
27 2 Kings 10:32–12:21; Acts 18:1–22; Psalm 145:1–21; Proverbs 18:1
28 2 Kings 13:1–14:29; Acts 18:23–19:12; Psalm 146:1–10; Proverbs 18:2–3
29 2 Kings 15:1–16:20; Acts 19:13–41; Psalm 147:1–20; Proverbs 18:4–5
30 2 Kings 17:1–18:12; Acts 20:1–38; Psalm 148:1–14; Proverbs 18:6–7

July

1 2 Kings 18:13–19:37; Acts 21:1–17; Psalm 149:1–9; Proverbs 18:8

2 2 Kings 20:1–22:2; Acts 21:18–36; Psalm 150:1–6; Proverbs 18:9–10

3 2 Kings 22:3–23:30; Acts 21:37–22:16; Psalm 1:1–6; Proverbs 18:11–12

4 2 Kings 23:31–25:30; Acts 22:17–23:10; Psalm 2:1–12; Proverbs 18:13

5 1 Chronicles 1:1–2:17; Acts 23:11–35; Psalm 3:1–8; Proverbs 18:14–15

6 1 Chronicles 2:18–4:4; Acts 24:1–27; Psalm 4:1–8; Proverbs 18:16–18

7 1 Chronicles 4:5–5:17; Acts 25:1–27; Psalm 5:1–12; Proverbs 18:19

8 1 Chronicles 5:18–6:81; Acts 26:1–32; Psalm 6:1–10; Proverbs 18:20–21

9 1 Chronicles 7:1–8:40; Acts 27:1–20; Psalm 7:1–17; Proverbs 18:22

10 1 Chronicles 9:1–10:14; Acts 27:21–44; Psalm 8:1–9; Proverbs 18:23–24

11 1 Chronicles 11:1–12:18; Acts 28:1–31; Psalm 9:1–12; Proverbs 19:1–3

12 1 Chronicles 12:19–14:17; Romans 1:1–17; Psalm 9:13–20; Proverbs 19:4–5

13 1 Chronicles 15:1–16:36; Romans 1:18–32; Psalm 10:1–15; Proverbs 19:6–7

14 1 Chronicles 16:37–18:17; Romans 2:1–24; Psalm 10:16–18; Proverbs 19:8–9

15 1 Chronicles 19:1–21:30; Romans 2:25–3:8; Psalm 11:1–7; Proverbs 19:10–12

16 1 Chronicles 22:1–23:32; Romans 3:9–31; Psalm 12:1–8; Proverbs 19:13–14

17 1 Chronicles 24:1–26:11; Romans 4:1–12; Psalm 13:1–6; Proverbs 19:15–16

18 1 Chronicles 26:12–27:34; Romans 4:13–5:5; Psalm 14:1–7; Proverbs 19:17

19 1 Chronicles 28:1–29:30; Romans 5:6–21; Psalm 15:1–5; Proverbs 19:18–19

20 2 Chronicles 1:1–3:17; Romans 6:1–23; Psalm 16:1–11; Proverbs 19:20–21

21 2 Chronicles 4:1–6:11; Romans 7:1–13; Psalm 17:1–15; Proverbs 19:22–23

22 2 Chronicles 6:12–8:10; Romans 7:14–8:8; Psalm 18:1–15; Proverbs 19:24–25

23 2 Chronicles 8:11–10:19; Romans 8:9–25; Psalm 18:16–36; Proverbs 19:26

24 2 Chronicles 11:1–13:22; Romans 8:26–39; Psalm 18:37–50; Proverbs 19:27–29

25 2 Chronicles 14:1–16:14; Romans 9:1–24; Psalm 19:1–14; Proverbs 20:1

26 2 Chronicles 17:1–18:34; Romans 9:25–10:13; Psalm 20:1–9; Proverbs 20:2–3

27 2 Chronicles 19:1–20:37; Romans 10:14–11:12; Psalm 21:1–13; Proverbs 20:4–6

28 2 Chronicles 21:1–23:21; Romans 11:13–36; Psalm 22:1–18; Proverbs 20:7

29 2 Chronicles 24:1–25:28; Romans 12:1–21; Psalm 22:19–31; Proverbs 20:8–10

30 2 Chronicles 26:1–28:27; Romans 13:1–14; Psalm 23:1–6; Proverbs 20:11

31 2 Chronicles 29:1–36; Romans 14:1–23; Psalm 24:1–10; Proverbs 20:12

August

1 2 Chronicles 30:1–31:21; Romans 15:1–22; Psalm 25:1–15; Proverbs 20:13–15
2 2 Chronicles 32:1–33:13; Romans 15:23–16:9; Psalm 25:16–22; Proverbs 20:16–18
3 2 Chronicles 33:14–34:33; Romans 16:10–27; Psalm 26:1–12; Proverbs 20:19
4 2 Chronicles 35:1–36:23; 1 Corinthians 1:1–17; Psalm 27:1–6; Proverbs 20:20–21
5 Ezra 1:1–2:70; 1 Corinthians 1:18–2:5; Psalm 27:7–14; Proverbs 20:22–23
6 Ezra 3:1–4:23; 1 Corinthians 2:6–3:4; Psalm 28:1–9; Proverbs 20:24–25
7 Ezra 4:24–6:22; 1 Corinthians 3:5–23; Psalm 29:1–11; Proverbs 20:26–27
8 Ezra 7:1–8:20; 1 Corinthians 4:1–21; Psalm 30:1–12; Proverbs 20:28–30
9 Ezra 8:21–9:15; 1 Corinthians 5:1–13; Psalm 31:1–8; Proverbs 21:1–2
10 Ezra 10:1–44; 1 Corinthians 6:1–20; Psalm 31:9–18; Proverbs 21:3
11 Nehemiah 1:1–3:14; 1 Corinthians 7:1–24; Psalm 31:19–24; Proverbs 21:4
12 Nehemiah 3:15–5:13; 1 Corinthians 7:25–40; Psalm 32:1–11; Proverbs 21:5–7
13 Nehemiah 5:14–7:73; 1 Corinthians 8:1–13; Psalm 33:1–11; Proverbs 21:8–10
14 Nehemiah 8:1–9:21; 1 Corinthians 9:1–18; Psalm 33:12–22; Proverbs 21:11–12
15 Nehemiah 9:22–10:39; 1 Corinthians 9:19–10:13; Psalm 34:1–10; Proverbs 21:13
16 Nehemiah 11:1–12:26; 1 Corinthians 10:14–33; Psalm 34:11–22; Proverbs 21:14–16
17 Nehemiah 12:27–13:31; 1 Corinthians 11:1–16; Psalm 35:1–16; Proverbs 21:17–18
18 Esther 1:1–3:15; 1 Corinthians 11:17–34; Psalm 35:17–28; Proverbs 21:19–20
19 Esther 4:1–7:10; 1 Corinthians 12:1–26; Psalm 36:1–12; Proverbs 21:21–22
20 Esther 8:1–10:3; 1 Corinthians 12:27–13:13; Psalm 37:1–11; Proverbs 21:23–24
21 Job 1:1–3:26; 1 Corinthians 14:1–17; Psalm 37:12–29; Proverbs 21:25–26
22 Job 4:1–7:21; 1 Corinthians 14:18–40; Psalm 37:30–40; Proverbs 21:27
23 Job 8:1–11:20; 1 Corinthians 15:1–28; Psalm 38:1–22; Proverbs 21:28–29
24 Job 12:1–15:35; 1 Corinthians 15:29–58; Psalm 39:1–13; Proverbs 21:30–31
25 Job 16:1–19:29; 1 Corinthians 16:1–24; Psalm 40:1–10; Proverbs 22:1
26 Job 20:1–22:30; 2 Corinthians 1:1–11; Psalm 40:11–17; Proverbs 22:2–4
27 Job 23:1–27:23; 2 Corinthians 1:12–2:11; Psalm 41:1–13; Proverbs 22:5–6
28 Job 28:1–30:31; 2 Corinthians 2:12–17; Psalm 42:1–11; Proverbs 22:7
29 Job 31:1–33:33; 2 Corinthians 3:1–18; Psalm 43:1–5; Proverbs 22:8–9
30 Job 34:1–36:33; 2 Corinthians 4:1–12; Psalm 44:1–8; Proverbs 22:10–12
31 Job 37:1–39:30; 2 Corinthians 4:13–5:10; Psalm 44:9–26; Proverbs 22:13

September

1 Job 40:1–42:17; 2 Corinthians 5:11–21; Psalm 45:1–17; Proverbs 22:14
2 Ecclesiastes 1:1–3:22; 2 Corinthians 6:1–13; Psalm 46:1–11; Proverbs 22:15
3 Ecclesiastes 4:1–6:12; 2 Corinthians 6:14–7:7; Psalm 47:1–9; Proverbs 22:16
4 Ecclesiastes 7:1–9:18; 2 Corinthians 7:8–16; Psalm 48:1–14; Proverbs 22:17–19
5 Ecclesiastes 10:1–12:14; 2 Corinthians 8:1–15; Psalm 49:1–20; Proverbs 22:20–21
6 Song of Solomon 1:1–4:16; 2 Corinthians 8:16–24; Psalm 50:1–23; Proverbs 22:22–23
7 Song of Solomon 5:1–8:14; 2 Corinthians 9:1–15; Psalm 51:1–19; Proverbs 22:24–25
8 Isaiah 1:1–2:22; 2 Corinthians 10:1–18; Psalm 52:1–9; Proverbs 22:26–27
9 Isaiah 3:1–5:30; 2 Corinthians 11:1–15; Psalm 53:1–6; Proverbs 22:28–29
10 Isaiah 6:1–7:25: 2 Corinthians 11:16–33; Psalm 54:1–7; Proverbs 23:1–3
11 Isaiah 8:1–9:21; 2 Corinthians 12:1–10; Psalm 55:1–23; Proverbs 23:4–5
12 Isaiah 10:1–11:16; 2 Corinthians 12:11–21; Psalm 56:1–13; Proverbs 23:6–8
13 Isaiah 12:1–14:32; 2 Corinthians 13:1–14; Psalm 57:1–11; Proverbs 23:9–11
14 Isaiah 15:1–18:7; Galatians 1:1–24; Psalm 58:1–11; Proverbs 23:12
15 Isaiah 19:1–21:17; Galatians 2:1–16; Psalm 59:1–17; Proverbs 23:13–14
16 Isaiah 22:1–24:23; Galatians 2:17–3:9; Psalm 60:1–12; Proverbs 23:15–16
17 Isaiah 25:1–28:13; Galatians 3:10–22; Psalm 61:1–8; Proverbs 23:17–18
18 Isaiah 28:14–30:11; Galatians 3:23–4:31; Psalm 62:1–12; Proverbs 23:19–21
19 Isaiah 30:12–33:9; Galatians 5:1–12; Psalm 63:1–11; Proverbs 23:22
20 Isaiah 33:10–36:22; Galatians 5:13–26; Psalm 64:1–10; Proverbs 23:23
21 Isaiah 37:1–38:22; Galatians 6:1–18; Psalm 65:1–13; Proverbs 23:24
22 Isaiah 39:1–41:16; Ephesians 1:1–23; Psalm 66:1–20; Proverbs 23:25–28
23 Isaiah 41:17–43:13; Ephesians 2:1–22; Psalm 67:1–7; Proverbs 23:29–35
24 Isaiah 43:14–45:10; Ephesians 3:1–21; Psalm 68:1–18; Proverbs 24:1–2
25 Isaiah 45:11–48:11; Ephesians 4:1–16; Psalm 68:19–35; Proverbs 24:3–4
26 Isaiah 48:12–50:11; Ephesians 4:17–32; Psalm 69:1–18; Proverbs 24:5–6
27 Isaiah 51:1–53:12; Ephesians 5:1–33; Psalm 69:19–36; Proverbs 24:7
28 Isaiah 54:1–57:14; Ephesians 6:1–24; Psalm 70:1–5; Proverbs 24:8
29 Isaiah 57:15–59:21; Philippians 1:1–26; Psalm 71:1–24; Proverbs 24:9–10
30 Isaiah 60:1–62:5; Philippians 1:27–2:18; Psalm 72:1–20; Proverbs 24:11–12

October

1 Isaiah 62:6–65:25; Philippians 2:19–3:3; Psalm 73:1–28; Proverbs 24:13–14

2 Isaiah 66:1–24; Philippians 3:4–21; Psalm 74:1–23; Proverbs 24:15–16

3 Jeremiah 1:1–2:30; Philippians 4:1–23; Psalm 75:1–10; Proverbs 24:17–20

4 Jeremiah 2:31–4:18; Colossians 1:1–17; Psalm 76:1–12; Proverbs 24:21–22

5 Jeremiah 4:19–6:15; Colossians 1:18–2:7; Psalm 77:1–20; Proverbs 24:23–25

6 Jeremiah 6:16–8:7; Colossians 2:8–23; Psalm 78:1–31; Proverbs 24:26

7 Jeremiah 8:8–9:26; Colossians 3:1–17; Psalm 78:32–55; Proverbs 24:27

8 Jeremiah 10:1–11:23; Colossians 3:18–4:18; Psalm 78:56–72; Proverbs 24:28–29

9 Jeremiah 12:1–14:10; 1 Thessalonians 1:1–2:8; Psalm 79:1–13; Proverbs 24:30–34

10 Jeremiah 14:11–16:15; 1 Thessalonians 2:9–3:13; Psalm 80:1–19; Proverbs 25:1–5

11 Jeremiah 16:16–18:23; 1 Thessalonians 4:1–5:3; Psalm 81:1–16; Proverbs 25:6–8

12 Jeremiah 19:1–21:14; 1 Thessalonians 5:4–28; Psalm 82:1–8; Proverbs 25:9–10

13 Jeremiah 22:1–23:20; 2 Thessalonians 1:1–12; Psalm 83:1–18; Proverbs 25:11–14

14 Jeremiah 23:21–25:38; 2 Thessalonians 2:1–17; Psalm 84:1–12; Proverbs 25:15

15 Jeremiah 26:1–27:22; 2 Thessalonians 3:1–18; Psalm 85:1–13; Proverbs 25:16

16 Jeremiah 28:1–29:32; 1 Timothy 1:1–20; Psalm 86:1–17; Proverbs 25:17

17 Jeremiah 30:1–31:26; 1 Timothy 2:1–15; Psalm 87:1–7; Proverbs 25:18–19

18 Jeremiah 31:27–32:44; 1 Timothy 3:1–16; Psalm 88:1–18; Proverbs 25:20–22

19 Jeremiah 33:1–34:22; 1 Timothy 4:1–16; Psalm 89:1–13; Proverbs 25:23–24

20 Jeremiah 35:1–36:32;1 Timothy 5:1–25; Psalm 89:14–37; Proverbs 25:25–27

21 Jeremiah 37:1–38:28; 1 Timothy 6:1–21; Psalm 89:38–52; Proverbs 25:28

22 Jeremiah 39:1–41:18; 2 Timothy 1:1–18; Psalm 90:1–91:16; Proverbs 26:1–2

23 Jeremiah 42:1–44:23; 2 Timothy 2:1–21; Psalm 92:1–93:5; Proverbs 26:3–5

24 Jeremiah 44:24–47:7; 2 Timothy 2:22–3:17; Psalm 94:1–23; Proverbs 26:6–8

25 Jeremiah 48:1–49:22; 2 Timothy 4:1–22; Psalm 95:1–96:13; Proverbs 26:9–12

26 Jeremiah 49:23–50:46; Titus 1:1–16; Psalm 97:1–98:9; Proverbs 26:13–16

27 Jeremiah 51:1–53; Titus 2:1–15; Psalm 99:1–9; Proverbs 26:17

28 Jeremiah 51:54–52:34; Titus 3:1–15; Psalm 100:1–5; Proverbs 26:18–19

29 Lamentations 1:1–2:22; Philemon 1:1–25; Psalm 101:1–8; Proverbs 26:20

30 Lamentations 3:1–66; Hebrews 1:1–14; Psalm 102:1–28; Proverbs 26:21–22

31 Lamentations 4:1–5:22; Hebrews 2:1–18; Psalm 103:1–22; Proverbs 26:23

November

1 Ezekiel 1:1–3:15; Hebrews 3:1–19; Psalm 104:1–23; Proverbs 26:24–26
2 Ezekiel 3:16–6:14; Hebrews 4:1–16; Psalm 104:24–35; Proverbs 26:27
3 Ezekiel 7:1–9:11; Hebrews 5:1–14; Psalm 105:1–15; Proverbs 26:28
4 Ezekiel 10:1–11:25; Hebrews 6:1–20; Psalm 105:16–36; Proverbs 27:1–2
5 Ezekiel 12:1–14:11; Hebrews 7:1–17; Psalm 105:37–45; Proverbs 27:3
6 Ezekiel 14:12–16:41; Hebrews 7:18–28; Psalm 106:1–12; Proverbs 27:4–6
7 Ezekiel 16:42–17:24; Hebrews 8:1–13; Psalm 106:13–31; Proverbs 27:7–9
8 Ezekiel 18:1–19:14; Hebrews 9:1–10; Psalm 106:32–48; Proverbs 27:10
9 Ezekiel 20:1–49; Hebrews 9:11–28; Psalm 107:1–43; Proverbs 27:11
10 Ezekiel 21:1–22:31; Hebrews 10:1–17; Psalm 108:1–13; Proverbs 27:12
11 Ezekiel 23:1–49; Hebrews 10:18–39; Psalm 109:1–31; Proverbs 27:13
12 Ezekiel 24:1–26:21; Hebrews 11:1–16; Psalm 110:1–7; Proverbs 27:14
13 Ezekiel 27:1–28:26; Hebrews 11:17–31; Psalm 111:1–10; Proverbs 27:15–16
14 Ezekiel 29:1–30:26; Hebrews 11:32–12:13; Psalm 112:1–10; Proverbs 27:17
15 Ezekiel 31:1–32:32; Hebrews 12:14–29; Psalm 113:1–114:8; Proverbs 27:18–20
16 Ezekiel 33:1–34:31; Hebrews 13:1–25; Psalm 115:1–18; Proverbs 27:21–22
17 Ezekiel 35:1–36:38; James 1:1–18; Psalm 116:1–19; Proverbs 27:23–27
18 Ezekiel 37:1–38:23; James 1:19–2:17; Psalm 117:1–2; Proverbs 28:1
19 Ezekiel 39:1–40:27; James 2:18–3:18; Psalm 118:1–18; Proverbs 28:2
20 Ezekiel 40:28–41:26; James 4:1–17; Psalm 118:19–29; Proverbs 28:3–5
21 Ezekiel 42:1–43:27; James 5:1–20; Psalm 119:1–16; Proverbs 28:6–7
22 Ezekiel 44:1–45:12; 1 Peter 1:1–12; Psalm 119:17–32; Proverbs 28:8–10
23 Ezekiel 45:13–46:24; 1 Peter 1:13–2:10; Psalm 119:33–48; Proverbs 28:11
24 Ezekiel 47:1–48:35; 1 Peter 2:11–3:7; Psalm 119:49–64; Proverbs 28:12–13
25 Daniel 1:1–2:23; 1 Peter 3:8–4:6; Psalm 119:65–80; Proverbs 28:14
26 Daniel 2:24–3:30; 1 Peter 4:7–5:14; Psalm 119:81–96; Proverbs 28:15–16
27 Daniel 4:1–37; 2 Peter 1:1–21; Psalm 119:97–112; Proverbs 28:17–18
28 Daniel 5:1–31; 2 Peter 2:1–22; Psalm 119:113–128; Proverbs 28:19–20
29 Daniel 6:1–28; 2 Peter 3:1–18; Psalm 119:129–152; Proverbs 28:21–22
30 Daniel 7:1–28; 1 John 1:1–10; Psalm 119:153–176; Proverbs 28:23–24

December

 1 Daniel 8:1–27; 1 John 2:1–17; Psalm 120:1–7; Proverbs 28:25–26
 2 Daniel 9:1–11:1; 1 John 2:18–3:6; Psalm 121:1–8; Proverbs 28:27–28
 3 Daniel 11:2–35; 1 John 3:7–24; Psalm 122:1–9; Proverbs 29:1
 4 Daniel 11:36–12:13; 1 John 4:1–21; Psalm 123:1–4; Proverbs 29:2–4
 5 Hosea 1:1–3:5; 1 John 5:1–21; Psalm 124:1–8; Proverbs 29:5–8
 6 Hosea 4:1–5:15; 2 John 1:1–13; Psalm 125:1–5; Proverbs 29:9–11
 7 Hosea 6:1–9:17; 3 John 1:1–15; Psalm 126:1–6; Proverbs 29:12–14
 8 Hosea 10:1–14:9; Jude 1:1–25; Psalm 127:1–5; Proverbs 29:15–17
 9 Joel 1:1–3:21; Revelation 1:1–20; Psalm 128:1–6; Proverbs 29:18
10 Amos 1:1–3:15; Revelation 2:1–17; Psalm 129:1–8; Proverbs 29:19–20
11 Amos 4:1–6:14; Revelation 2:18–3:6; Psalm 130:1–8; Proverbs 29:21–22
12 Amos 7:1–9:15; Revelation 3:7–22; Psalm 131:1–3; Proverbs 29:23
13 Obadiah 1:1–21; Revelation 4:1–11; Psalm 132:1–18; Proverbs 29:24–25
14 Jonah 1:1–4:11; Revelation 5:1–14; Psalm 133:1–3; Proverbs 29:26–27
15 Micah 1:1–4:13; Revelation 6:1–17; Psalm 134:1–3; Proverbs 30:1–4
16 Micah 5:1–7:20; Revelation 7:1–17; Psalm 135:1–21; Proverbs 30:5–6
17 Nahum 1:1–3:19; Revelation 8:1–13; Psalm 136:1–26; Proverbs 30:7–9
18 Habakkuk 1:1–3:19; Revelation 9:1–21; Psalm 137:1–9; Proverbs 30:10
19 Zephaniah 1:1–3:20; Revelation 10:1–11; Psalm 138:1–8; Proverbs 30:11–14
20 Haggai 1:1–2:23; Revelation 11:1–19; Psalm 139:1–24; Proverbs 30:15–16
21 Zechariah 1:1–21; Revelation 12:1–17; Psalm 140:1–13; Proverbs 30:17
22 Zechariah 2:1–3:10; Revelation 13:1–18; Psalm 141:1–10; Proverbs 30:18–20
23 Zechariah 4:1–5:11; Revelation 14:1–20; Psalm 142:1–7; Proverbs 30:21–23
24 Zechariah 6:1–7:14; Revelation 15:1–8; Psalm 143:1–12; Proverbs 30:24–28
25 Zechariah 8:1–23; Revelation 16:1–21; Psalm 144:1–15; Proverbs 30:29–31
26 Zechariah 9:1–17; Revelation 17:1–18; Psalm 145:1–21; Proverbs 30:32
27 Zechariah 10:1–11:17; Revelation 18:1–24; Psalm 146:1–10; Proverbs 30:33
28 Zechariah 12:1–13:9; Revelation 19:1–21; Psalm 147:1–20; Proverbs 31:1–7
29 Zechariah 14:1–21; Revelation 20:1–15; Psalm 148:1–14; Proverbs 31:8–9
30 Malachi 1:1–2:17; Revelation 21:1–27; Psalm 149:1–9; Proverbs 31:10–24
31 Malachi 3:1–4:6; Revelation 22:1–21; Psalm 150:1–6; Proverbs 31:25–31

Also look for *My Pocket Prayer Partner for Women.*

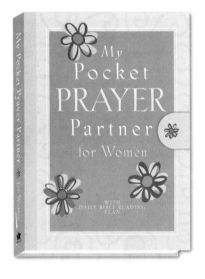